PLACES TO GO
WITH CHILDREN
in
Northern California

ELIZABETH POMADA

CHRONICLE BOOKS SAN FRANCISCO

LIBRARY OF CONGRESS CATALOGING IN PUBLICATION DATA

Pomada, Elizabeth.
  Places to go with children in Northern California.

  Includes index.
  1. California, Northern—Description and travel—
Guide-books. 2. Family recreation—California,
Northern.
  I. Title.
F867.5.P66 1985   917.94   85-3804
ISBN 0-87701-328-4

Editing: Deborah Stone
Typography: Harrington-Young
Book and Cover Design: Fearn Cutler
Cover Photograph: Mark Gibson

10 9 8 7 6 5 4 3 2 1
Chronicle Books
One Hallidie Plaza
San Francisco, CA 94102

PHOTO CREDITS

*E.R. Susse p.17, 22, 50, 54, 62, 70, 85, 93, 108;
Courtesy of Hyde Street Pier (GGNRA) p. 8; Hanford
Associates p. 12; California Academy of Sciences p. 20;
Michael Larsen p. 26, 35, 66, 96, 132; Courtesy of Old
Faithful Geyser p.28; Courtesy of Sterling Vineyards p. 31;
Courtesy of State of California Department of Parks and
Recreation p. 38, 110, 134, 137; Courtesy of U.S. Coast
Guard p. 40; Edward Freitas p. 43; Pat Derby p. 45; Cour-
tesy of San Mateo County Convention and Visitors Bureau
p. 57; World of Miniatures p. 64; Courtesy of Roaring
Camp Railroad p. 69; Fearn Cutler p. 73; Courtesy of The
Steinbeck House p. 79; Karen R. Preuss p. 82; Charles
Frizzel Photography p. 90; Courtesy of Sacramento Conven-
tion and Visitors Bureau p. 101; Courtesy of Silver Wings
Aviation Museum p. 104; Courtesy of Sierra Railway p.
113; Courtesy of Mercer Caverns p. 115; Bob Anderson p.
122; Forestiere Gardens p. 128; U.S. Department of the In-
terior p. 130; Tom Myers p. 141; State of California Department of Beaches and Parks p. 142; Courtesy of San
Mateo County Convention and Visitors Bureau p. 149.*

Needless to say, this book was not done by just one person. I must say "Thank you" to Lauren and Jennifer, Elizabeth and Deborah, Diana and Marc, Eric and Chris, Cindy and Christopher and Alan, our "test" children. But most of all, thank you to my editor, chauffeur, idea man, hero, and the biggest child of them all—MFL.

E.P.

CONTENTS

INTRODUCTION

To research the first edition of PLACES TO GO WITH CHIL-
DREN IN NORTHERN CALIFORNIA, we explored, read books,
and drove over most of Northern California, searching out places
that would be educational, historical, and, as the Pollardville Ghost
Town billboard put it, "entertational." We believe that if you and
your children can learn something and have fun at the same time,
then the good time is worth twice as much. Most of the places listed
here are enjoyable no matter how old you are.

Traveling through Northern California you'll find a wonderfully varied, beautiful country—and learn the history of the state
at the same time. This book concentrates on places to go, rather than
on things to do, so we haven't included the usual activities youngsters like, such as bowling, skateboarding, skiing, pool, skating,
go-carting, miniature golf, ballooning, and ice skating. Nor have we
included all the national, state, county, and city parks.

We give special emphasis to year-round attractions—and to those
that are free. There are some well-known tourist attractions that
were left out because we feel they are either not suitable or not especially enjoyable for children.

Museums, steam railroads, natural wonders, special restaurants
that appeal to youngsters, and man-made amusements are all here
for you to try—along with a list of festivals, fairs, and feasts that are
annual happenings.

Local Chambers of Commerce, tourist offices, or a telephone
call can give you up-to-the-minute times, prices, and dates, as well as
lodging and driving information. Most attractions are privately
owned and subject to changes in schedules and prices at any time.
Most places are closed on Christmas, Thanksgiving, and New Year's
Day. All chapters are planned so that you can drive from place to
place in order, radiating out from San Francisco. Do call first if
you're going a long way.

We'd like to hear about special places you and your children discover. In the meantime, equipped with this book and your imagination, you and your children are sure to have a glorious time. Enjoy!

SAN FRANCISCO

What is the secret of San Francisco's attraction? A combination of natural beauty, a short but lively history in which gold and disaster loom large, and a dynamic mixture of peoples and cultures: Hispanic, Chinese, Italian, Russian, French, Japanese. Together, these elements have made a magnet that attracts visitors from all over the world.

San Francisco is a center for culture (and counterculture), business, education, entertainment, and tourism. The City provides a lot to see and do for children and their parents. And those formidable hills notwithstanding, the best way for a family to do it is on foot (with sweaters on hand in case of fog or winds). So pick an area and a destination, park the car or get off one of the ubiquitous buses, and start walking!

For openers, we suggest taking a cable car to the Fairmont Hotel on Nob Hill, and the free ride on its outside elevator to the Crown Room at the top. Night or day, the view is spectacular. From there, walk through North Beach, with its exciting Italian delicatessens, to the Bay, where you'll find something for everyone. For a 360-degree view of the Bay and the City, stop by at Coit Tower on the top of Telegraph Hill. The observation platform at the top of the tower is 210 feet high (open daily, 9 to 4:30).

On the other side of town, the first twelve blocks of Clement Street is the heart of the Russian District. Nosh a piroshki, a tasty meat-filled pastry, as you wander through neighborhood stores. The Mission District offers Latin American groceries and a multitude of Mexican delights. For kids, just as for adults, the neighborhoods of San Francisco offer glimpses of other cultures.

And as my nephew Alan says "Just riding the cable cars up and down hills and looking is the best thing to do."

GOLDEN GATE FERRY TO LARKSPUR OR SAUSALITO

Next to the Ferry Building (at the foot of Market Street). (415) 332-6600. Ferries leave the City daily, at 1½ hour intervals. Call for schedule. Sausalito: Adults, $2.75; children, $2.05. Larkspur: Adults, $2.25; children, $1.65.

The Golden Gate Ferry leaves its slip at the foot of Market Street, passes Alcatraz Island, and docks across the bay. The shop on board serves good coffee and snacks—and the views are wonderful!

VAILLANCOURT FOUNTAIN

Embarcadero Plaza, at the foot of Market Street. Free.
When the water in this bizarre, poured-concrete fountain is turned off, it "looks like it was hit by an earthquake but didn't fall all the way down." But when the water is running and you can walk over, under, and around rushing falls and streams, it's another story. Embarcadero Plaza hosts an informal crafts fair on weekday lunch hours and on weekends. Next door, the Hyatt Regency offers a spectacular twenty-first century lobby to wander around, with a fountain, a burbling brook, and glass elevators that travel—up to the top of the lobby—twenty stories above.

DOLPHIN P. REMPP SHIPBOARD RESTAURANT

Embarcadero and Berry, Second Street, Pier 42. (415) 777-5771/957-1470. Lunch and dinner daily.
The three-masted, 155-foot long cargo schooner *Ellen* has been transformed to a flag-flying restaurant perched on San Francisco's Embarcadero. A nautical bar and stainless steel galley serve fresh seafood and drinks to people who like to "pretend cruise" while they dine.

A WORLD OF OIL/CHEVRON USA

555 Market Street. (415) 894-4895. Monday–Friday. 9:30–4. Tours by appointment. Films weekdays at noon. Free.
If you've ever wondered how oil is found, produced, transformed into thousands of products, and used for energy, heat, and lubrication, this is the place to come. A short film shows how tremendous amounts of time and underground pressure change decomposing plants and animals into petroleum, and how oil was obtained and used in the past. The search for black gold is illustrated with photos, models of rigs, actual drilling tools, and a mural of a modern refining plant. Three life-size dioramas show the role oil has played in American life. One with particular appeal for children shows a family in a 1910 kitchen.

THE OLD MINT

Fifth and Mission Streets. (415) 974-0788. Tuesday–Saturday, 10–4. 1½ hour guided tours by appointment. Closed on holidays. Free.
A half-hour film, "The Granite Lady," unfolds this history of California and the part the Old Mint played in it, from the crackling excitement of the Gold Rush to the terror of the earthquake and fire. Visitors can see tokens, notes, walrus and seal skins, and other forms of money as well as a stack of 128 gold bars, and gold nuggets. In one of the restored rooms, the superin-

tendent's office, the clock reads "Time is Money." Visitors can strike their own souvenir medal on a 1869 coil press.

LYLE TUTTLE'S TATTOO MUSEUM

30 Seventh Street. (415) 864-9798. Tuesday–Saturday, 12–6. Free.

Thousands of tattoos, designs, and instruments, including a Boer War (1898) tattoo pattern and pre-Columbian tattoo devices, makes this one of the most unusual museums in the world.

THE ASAWA FOUNTAIN

Hyatt Hotel on Union Square, Stockton Street, between Sutter and Post. Free.

Ruth Asawa, creator of the Mermaid Fountain in Ghirardelli Square, has given the people of San Francisco a one-stop tour of the people and places that make up the City. This round (14 feet in diameter) fountain, on the steps of the hotel's plaza, was molded in bread dough—the same dough children use for sculpting—and cast in bronze. And the little people, trees, Chinese dragon, gingerbread houses, and school buses demand to be touched. If you stand at the bottom of the fountain, you'll find the Ferry Building; then as you go around the fountain counterclockwise, you'll see Coit Tower, Broadway, Maritime Park, the Cannery, the zoo, the Mission District—everything laid out in the same general direction as it is in real life. A group of Noe Valley schoolchildren created one of the fountain's forty-one plaques, which depicts the children of San Francisco. Your children will enjoy figuring out which one it is.

MUSEUM OF MONEY OF THE AMERICAN WEST

Bank of California, 400 California Street, downstairs. (415) 765-0400. Monday–Thursday, 10–3; Friday until 5. Free.

This small but beautifully mounted collection of money and gold provides intriguing glimpses of banking and mining in the Old West. Privately minted coins from Utah, Colorado, and California illustrate the kind of money used before the U.S. Mint was established in San Francisco. Ingots, bullion, fiscal paper, currency, and early bank drafts are here, along with counterfeit coins and counterfeit detectors. (One method of counterfeiting was "the platinum menace,"—hollowing coins and filling them with platinum, which was then worth much less than gold.) A new addition to the museum's collection is the pair of pistols used in a duel between David S. Terry and David C. Broderick in 1859.

WELLS FARGO HISTORY ROOM

420 Montgomery Street.(415) 396-2619. Banking days, 10–3. Free.

A Wells Fargo Concord Stagecoach is the centerpiece of this history of

Wells Fargo and the Old West. Treasure boxes and the old money, iron doors from the Wells Fargo building in the gold-country town of Chinese Camp, samples of gold, a map of Black Bart's twenty-eight stagecoach robberies (the story goes that he was always polite to women), and many other items provide details of Western history. Early photographic methods are illustrated, with sample photos and cameras and the high seat and iron headrest used for daguerrotypes. There's even a Buffalo Bill collection, along with a huge collection of stamps and postmarks.

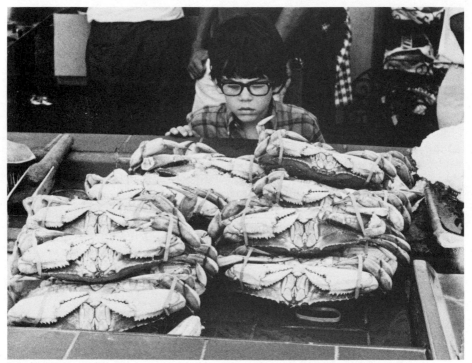

San Francisco—Chinatown

CHINATOWN

Walking through Chinatown can be like walking in another country or it can simply be a shopping trip, depending upon your mood. For the curious, there are fortune cookie factories, fish stores, and temples. Fortune cookie making is not a romantic process. A row of tiny griddles revolves under a hose that squirts dough onto each pan. The pans continue their circle, cooking the dough on their way to the fortune cookie-maker. She picks up the browned wafer, pushes it onto a spur to give it the first fold, inserts the paper fortune, presses the final fold, and puts the cookie into a muffin tin to harden. Golden Gate Fortune Cookie Company (23 Ross Alley, above Grant, between Washington and Jackson, 781-3956) frequently leaves their doors open so you can poke your head in to see the process in action. If you plan to go as a group, make an appointment. The King Chow Temple (Clay and Stockton, above the post office on the fourth floor) is the oldest Chinese family association in the U.S. Visiting hours are posted on the door. T'ien Hou Miao Temple (125 Waverly Place, fourth floor, 10–5 and 7–9 P.M. daily) is dedicated to the Queen of Heaven and boasts a ceiling filled with carved wood mythological figures. In nearby Portsmouth Square, there's a small wooden house leading to one of the best slides in the city.

CHINESE CULTURAL FOUNDATION

750 Kearny, in the Holiday Inn (415) 986-1822. Rotating exhibits and changing schedule. Free.

Cultural, historical and artistic exhibitions are presented in this forum for Chinese and Chinese-Americans.

YANK SING RESTAURANT

671 Broadway. 781-1111. Daily, 10–5.

Yank Sing is our favorite *dim sum* restaurant. *Dim sum*, also called Chinese tea or Chinese breakfast, means "heart's delights," and is one of the nicest ways I know of to have brunch. *Dim sum* is simply little bites of good things. A waitress or waiter comes around with a huge tray, from which you choose small plates of such delicacies as steamed pork buns, curry cakes, beef dumplings, shrimp rolls, black-bean sauce spareribs, and barbecued pork sandwiches. You pay by the number of plates piled up on your table, so if a dish like shrimp balls comes on two plates, and there are just 2 or 3 or you, you can ask for half an order, or one plate's worth. That way you'll have more room to try more "heart's delights." Other *dim sum* places we can recommend are the Hong Kong Tea Garden, Golden Dragon, and Grand Palace.

CHINESE HISTORICAL SOCIETY OF AMERICA

17 Adler Place (between Grant and Columbus, just south of Broadway), (415) 391-1188. Tuesday–Saturday, 1–5. Donation.

Chinese societies throughout California have contributed to this small, almost hidden museum to show how Chinese contributed to California's development. Ceremonial swords, printing blocks, an altar block, porcelain pillows, clothes worn by nineteenth century high-born and laborers, opium pipes, photos, and documents crowd the walls.

NORTH BEACH MUSEUM

1435 Stockton, upstairs in Eureka Federal Savings Bank. (415) 391-6210. Monday–Thursday, 9–4:30; Friday until 6; Saturday, 9–3. Tours by appointment: 334-4600. Free.

Photographs and artifacts in changing thematic exhibits rejoice in the City's, particularly North Beach's, colorful past, from the Gold Rush to the Earthquake to the Beat Generation. On our last visit, we saw an exhibit of San Francisco's mayors, from the *alcaldes* of the 1830s to the present.

MUSEO ITALIO AMERICANO

678 Green. (415) 398-2660. Wednesday-Sunday. 12–5 and by appointment. Free.

Italian and Italo-American culture are the focal points here. Exhibits of visual and audiovisuals show Italian-American contributors to art, architecture, design, cinema, music, and photography. Educational programs provide an insight on the influence of Italians and Italian-Americans on American life. Changing exhibits include ancient Roman artifacts and nineteenth and twentieth century art by artists such as Beniamino Bufano and Frank Stella.

CABLE CAR BARN MUSEUM

Washington and Mason Streets. (415) 474-1887. Daily, 10–5:45. Closed holidays. Donation.

All three cable car lines in San Francisco are run by the huge revolving red and yellow wheels in the brick cable car barn, built in 1887, now completely refurbished. Visitors can watch the wheels from a gallery, where there are samples of the cable itself and charts explaining how the cable cars work. Scale models, earthquake mementos, old cable car seats, and photographs mix with the cable cars on display, including the first one to operate in San Francisco, in 1873. An exciting new underground viewing room lets you see the cables running under the city streets from the car barn at 9½ miles an hour.

PIONEER HALL, SOCIETY OF CALIFORNIA PIONEERS

456 McAllister Street. (415) 861-5278. Monday–Friday, 10–4. Closed holidays and during August. (Children under 16 must be with adult.) Free.

Photos of the 1906 San Francisco earthquake and fire and the 1915 Exposition fill rack after rack in this long room. There is also a free slide show about the earthquake. Artifacts of the gold miners, of the transcontinental railroad and the driving of the Golden Spike, and menus used in early railroad dining cars are in wall cases. The Vigilance Committee bell, Vallejo's campaign chest, artifacts from the Niantic, fire trumpets, and an old stagecoach are among the other items of interest.

SAN FRANCISCO MUSEUM OF MODERN ART

War Memorial Veterans Building, Van Ness at McAllister. (415) 863-8800. Tuesday, Wednesday and Friday, 10–6; Thursday until 10 P.M.; weekends, 10–5. Closed holidays. Adults, $3; under 16, $1.50. Group rates.

The modern art museum constantly changes its exhibits of paintings, sculpture, works of art on paper, and photography. During a recent visit, we saw a dazzling collection of American abstract art. The Museum of Modern Art specializes in modern European and American paintings, sculpture, graphics, photography, and ceramics.

HAAS-LILIENTHAL HOUSE

2007 Franklin (between Washington & Jackson). (415) 441-3004. Guided tours Wednesday 12–4, Sunday 11-4:30. Adults: $3; students, seniors: $1

This glorious Queen Anne Victorian, built in 1886, is a completely furnished memory of yesteryear. Children of all ages will especially enjoy the train room.

HIPPO HAMBURGERS

2025 Van Ness (415) 771-3939. Sunday–Thursday 11:30 A.M.–1 A.M. Friday and Saturday until 3 A.M.

There are fifty-five kinds of hamburgers to choose from in this cheerful, circus-like restaurant. There are Italian burgers, onion burgers, Hawaiian burgers, Tahitian burgers, and spaghetti burgers at prices ranging from $3.50. The children's menu offers a Giraffeburger, Rhinoburger, and Gorrillaburger. Sandwiches, guacamole, divine fried onion rings, and good desserts such as warm banana fritters topped with hot cinnamon sauce, round out the menu. The adventurous might try the Hamburger sundae—a roll-less hamburger smothered in ice cream, hot fudge, chopped nuts, a cherry, and a pickle. Hippo bibs, lollipops, and balloons are there for the asking, and birthday boys and girls will be energetically sung to.

GHIRARDELLI CHOCOLATE MANUFACTORY

Ghirardelli Square, North Point and Polk. (415) 771-4903. 11:30 A.M.–10 P.M. daily.

Since the beginning of the century, Ghirardelli Stone-Ground Chocolate has been a popular trade name throughout the West. This red brick, aromatic ice cream and candy shop invokes that name in a nostalgic corner of the old Ghirardelli factory. After filling out an order form and paying the cashier, you locate a marble-topped table, then take turns watching the chocolate-making machinery in the back of the room until your order number is called. The Emperor Norton and Golden Gate Banana Splits are $4. Twin Peaks is chocolate and vanilla ice cream under marshmallow and chocolate sauce, covered with a whipped cream fog. The best buy may be the hot chocolate ($1.50), a large mug of ambrosial chocolate topped with melting marshmallows or whipped cream.

  Ghirardelli Square is a nice place to spend an afternoon. You can browse through Japanese, Dutch, Irish, Mexican, Greek, and American stores; taste almonds, watch street artists, delight in the kite store, dine in Indian, Mandarin, Hungarian or Italian restaurants, or just sit and watch the sailboats on the bay.

NATIONAL MARITIME MUSEUM AT SAN FRANCISCO (GGNRA)

Foot of Polk Street. (415) 556-8177. Daily 10–5, until 6 in summer. Free.

  The Maritime Museum is a mecca for ship lovers of all ages. The maritime history of San Francisco lives here in models of clippers, British iron ships, schooners, barkentines, cutters, cod fishers; and in photos, figureheads, tools, scrimshaw, guns and harpoons, diaries, and ships' logs. The 19-foot sloop *Mermaid*, which one man sailed from Osaka to San Francisco, is on the porch. Billy Bones, Blackbeard, Mary Read, and Anne Bonny are some of the pirates standing at the entrance to the Steamship Room. Inside, you'll find models of the *Queen Mary* and various cargo and warships from World War I to the present. The National Maritime Museum is part of the huge

On Board the C. A. Thayer—*Hyde Street Pier*

Golden Gate National Recreation Area or GGNRA run by the National Park Service.

SAN FRANCISCO HISTORIC SHIPS AT HYDE STREET PIER (GGNRA)

Hyde Street Pier. (415) 556-6435. Daily 10–5, open longer hours in summer. Tours and Environmental Living Programs by appointment. Free.

Plastic wands tell you about the ships, with narrations dramatized by sounds of creaking timbers, whistles, and the cries of seagulls as you climb aboard a sailing lumbership or the last paddle-wheel ferry to operate on San Francisco Bay. The *C. A. Thayer* operated here as a salmon packet and then as a codfisher. You can go below decks to see the captain's cabin (he sometimes brought his wife) and the galley, and then get behind the wheel. The *Eureka* features a display of antique cars and trucks on her lower deck. Upstairs, there's a newsstand stocked with all of the 1920 magazines and candies. Our favorite thing is the old nickelodeon. For 25¢ you can dance through the cavernous, empty vessel to the tunes of yesteryear. Just added to the pier are *The Alma*, the last remaining San Francisco Bay scow schooner, and *Hercules*, a 1907 oceangoing steam tug. The Tubbs Building, a cordage company, is being restored. Films, including "The Last Voyage of the *C. A. Thayer*," recount maritime history in the Tubbs Cordage Building.

GUINNESS MUSEUM OF WORLD RECORDS

235 Jefferson. (415) 771-9890. Sunday–Thursday, 10–10, Friday and Saturday until 12. Adults, $4.95; 12 and under, $2.50.

World records from the Guinness Book of World Records come to life in this fascinating museum. One can enjoy actual record-setting objects, exciting audience participation displays, stunning record dramatizations, and amazing multi-media videotapes and films of records being actually set. A trip through the museum can be both fun and educational.

RIPLEY'S BELIEVE IT OR NOT! MUSEUM

175 Jefferson. (415) 771 6188. Sunday–Thursday, 10–10; Friday and Saturday until 12. Adults, $4.95; under 12, $2.50.

Over twenty-five hundred oddities and puzzles are displayed along the Crooked Lane that leads you through this amusing collection. A man with four pupils in his eyes, another covered in chains, and another with a hole in his head gave us pause, as did the two-headed goat, the log cabin made with Lincoln pennies, and the display of "dressed" fleas. A perfect place to spend a rainy afternoon.

THE DESSERT COMPANY OF SAN FRANCISCO

The Cannery, 2801 Leavenworth. (415) 928-4503. Sunday–Thursday, 11–11; until 12 on weekends.

The Cannery itself is an old fish cannery remodeled into a galaxy of shops, a movie theater, a gourmet food shop, and restaurants. Street musicians and a glass elevator in the courtyard add to the youngsters' enjoyment of the place. Ice cream concoctions and tempting desserts taste better here because of the dazzling view before you—the bay from Berkeley to the Golden Gate Bridge.

WAX MUSEUM AT FISHERMAN'S WHARF

145 Jefferson. (415) 885-4975. Daily 10–10, longer hours in summer. Adults, $5.95; seniors and military, $4; children, $2.95.

Four levels of 275 figurines in 74 scenes vie for your attention here. Princess Grace, Queen Elizabeth, and Emperor Hirohito pay court to the visitor, as do stars such as John Lennon, Michael Jackson, Marilyn Monroe, Elvis Presley, and people from fables, like Peter Pan and Snow White. John Sutter drinks in an 1848 saloon, while Emperor Norton broods in a corner.

The Haunted Gold Mine (145 Jefferson Street; daily 9–11 in summer, 10–10 in winter; adults $3.50, seniors and military $2.50, children $1.75) is a splendid fun house filled with illusions, puzzles, and surprises. Don't think you're really walking into an old gold mine!

THE ENCHANTED WORLD OF OLD SAN FRANCISCO

Jefferson and Mason Streets. (415) 885-4834. Daily 10–10, later in summer. Groups by appointment. Adults, $2.50; seniors and military, $1.75; children, $1.25. Under 6 free.

Follow the red brick road to the pretty cable car and ride through San Francisco's history. One hundred and fifty animated characters sing to you as you travel through the Gold Rush days to the building of the City, to the Barbary Coast, to the scary 1906 earthquake and fire, and finally to the elegant Panama–Pacific Exposition and fireworks!

BALCLUTHA (GGNRA)

Pier 43. (415) 982-1886. Daily 9 A.M.–10:30 P.M. Adults, $2; ages 12–17, $1; 6–12, 25¢ (with parent, free).

One of the last surviving square-rigged Cape Horners, the *Balclutha* once flew twenty-five sails on its seventeen trips 'round the Horn. Today, you can spin the wheel, visit the "slop chest" and galley, check out the captain's quarters with its plush red settee and swinging bed, ring bells, and read sea chanties and rousing tales of the Barbary Coast in the museum downstairs. The rolling of the boat on the water adds just the right touch to your imaginary cruise.

The USS *Pampanito*, a World War II submarine (Pier 45; 673-0700; daily

10–10; adults $3, children $1.50) is a great adventure for armchair sailors.

COMMODORE HELICOPTER TOURS

*Pier 43. (415) 981-4832; Mill Valley office: 332-4482. Daily 10 A.M. to sunset, wea-
ther permitting. Adults, $12; under 10, $6; for four minute Bell Jet Ranger Ride.
Charter rates available.*

This exciting 125 mph ride swoops around Alcatraz, out onto the bay,
and over the City for some great views. Be sure to bring your camera. There
are four tours to choose from.

Seaplane flights are also available from the Marin Heliport (332-4843)
and there are other helicopter flights from China Basin (495-3333).

ALCATRAZ ISLAND (GGNRA)

*Pier 41. (415) 546-2805. Tours every 45 minutes. 8:45–2:45 in winter, until 5 in
summer. Adults, $3.50; ages 5–11, $2; tickets sold on a first come, first served basis.
Reservations can be made through Ticketron: adults, $4.25; ages 5–11, $2.75.
Groups rates available. Allow two hours for the ride and tour.*

Wear walking shoes and bring a sweater on this educational, fascinating-
yet-depressing tour. One friend calls the tour a sure-fire way to stop juvenile
delinquency.

Oceanic Society Expeditions (474-3385, by reservation) takes you on
day-long teaching trips to the Farallon Islands, weekends in summer.

BAY CRUISE

*Pier 43½. (415) 546-2810. Tours begin at 10 A.M. daily, weather permitting. Adults,
$8; ages 5–11, $4.*

On a sunny day in San Francisco, there's nothing nicer for all of the
family than the 75-minute cruise on San Francisco Bay. The guide points out
special sites and buildings and tells their story, but the really important thing
is the passage around that beautiful bay. You go from bridge to bridge, past
Alcatraz, and along the Embarcadero.

Harbor Tours leave Pier 41 to Sausalito 5 times a day, arriving 35 minutes later and returning to San Francisco seven times a day. The first boats
start later on weekends and holidays. Round-trip: adults, $6; ages 5–11, $3.

Harbor Tours also offer Sunday brunch cruises from April to October,
at 10:30 and 12:30, weather permitting, by reservation.

For a barbecue cruise on San Francisco Bay, call (415) 546-2803 for reservations.

TIBURON–ANGEL ISLAND STATE PARK FERRIES

Pier 43½. (415) 546-2815. Round trip: adults, $6; ages 5–11, $3.
The Red and White Fleet crosses the Bay from Fisherman's Wharf to

the romantic inlet at Angel Island. A snack bar is available, but most people spend the time on board staring at the bay and the seagulls following. For a description of Angel Island, see Marin County chapter.

PIER 39

The Embarcadero. (415) 981-PIER. Shops: 10:30–8:30; restaurants, 11:30–11:30.

The entire family will enjoy the Palace of Fun Arts which welcomes you to Pier 39. Here you'll find bumper cars, a new two-story carousel, and an arcade with games of skill and machines to play. The kids can spend hours here while you shop in the stores. There are jugglers and street entertainers to amuse you. Windsurfing and sailing lessons are available, or you can rent a boat yourself (School of Sailing, 421-8353) or take a scenic one-and-one-quarter hour Bay cruise on the Blue & Gold Fleet (781-7877). Take a horse-and-buggy or stagecoach ride. *The Rendezvous*, a square rigged tall ship, offers sails on the bay (885-1155). There are twenty-three restaurants to choose from: Mexican, Japanese, Chinese, Italian, Swiss, and fish of every kind, all with fabulous views of the bay.

Cherry Blossom Festival—San Francisco Japantown

THE SAN FRANCISCO EXPERIENCE

Pier 39. (415) 982-7394. Daily, 10–10. Adults, $3; seniors, military and ages 5–16, $2; 1 hour free parking in Pier 39 garage.

Seven screens, 32 speakers, three movie projectors, and 32 slide projectors bring you the spirit and history of San Francisco, from the gold mines to the building of the Golden Gate Bridge. Experience the San Francisco earthquake of 1906 and a Chinese New Year's Parade. The San Francisco memorabilia, nickelodeons, and games make waiting in the lobby for the next show a pleasure.

SAN FRANCISCO FIRE DEPARTMENT PIONEER MEMORIAL MUSEUM

655 Presidio, between Pine and Bush. (415) 558-3981. Thursday–Sunday, 1–4 and by appointment. Free.

Awe-inspiring photos of today's firefighters mingle with uniforms, bells, trophies and mementos of men and machines, the silver speaking trumpet, leather buckets, a buffalo-leather firehose and other relics of yesteryear. Lillie Coit, the darling of the San Francisco Fire Department, has her own case full of mementos. A 1912 fire chief's buggy, an Ahrens-Fox Piston Pumper, and an 1890 American LaFrance Steam Fire Engine fill the room.

THE WHITTIER MANSION

2090 Jackson Street.(415) 567-1848. Wednesday, Saturday and Sunday, 1–5 and by appointment. Adults, $2; students and seniors, $1; first Saturday of the month free.

The 1896 Whittier Mansion features revolving exhibits of California art. En route to the second floor exhibit area, you pass through gracious drawing rooms with parquet floors, handsome fireplaces, and carved wainscotting. The California Historical Society offers changing exhibits on the history, arts, and culture of California.

JAPAN CENTER

Post and Buchanan Streets. (415) 922-6776.

The Peace Plaza, with its reflecting pools and five-tiered Peace Pagoda, is the center of many entertaining happenings through the year: festivals; music and dance programs; judo, karate, and kendo matches. Inside, you can fish for an oyster with a pearl in it; have a Japanese fish-shaped pastry for dessert; and wander through bonsai, paper, gift, and book shops. The nearby blocks are filled with interesting hardware and grocery stores, tempura and sushi bars. Samarai movies and theatrical programs that will attract older children are scheduled in the corner theater. Japan Center, Nihonmachi, can really be another world. Japantown Bowl is across the street.

FORT MASON

Marina Boulevard at Laguna, (415) 441-5705.

The Golden Gate National Recreation Area is in the process of restoring Fort Mason to active use. Thirty-five nonprofit organizations reside here offering free or low-cost concerts, lectures, classes, children's hours, and many support services. The San Francisco Museum of Modern Art has a wing here. Greens is an elegant vegetarian restaurant run by the Zen Center of San Francisco offering creative pastas and barbecues, salads picked each day at the center's Green Gulch Farm, and breads and cakes from the Tassajara Bread Bakery. It has a phemonenal view of the docks, the bay, and Golden Gate Bridge (call 771-6222, lunch and dinner).

SS *JEREMIAH O'BRIEN* LIBERTY SHIP

Fort Mason, Pier 3 East. (415) 441-3101. 9–3 daily, free. Tours by appointment.

Launched June 19, 1943, the *Jeremiah O'Brien* carried food and ammunition to England, ferried troops during the Normandy invasion, and transported supplies to the South Pacific. Background movies and tapes augment your self-guided tour. The ship has been restored, preserved, and shared with the public by volunteers.

MEXICAN MUSEUM

Fort Mason Center, Building D. (415) 621-1244. Wednesday–Sunday, 12–5. Donation.

Pre-Hispanic, contemporary, and folk art by Mexicans and Chicanos make up the changing exhibits in this fine museum. The museum sponsors a walking tour of the Mission District's murals.

SAN FRANCISCO AFRICAN-AMERICAN HISTORICAL AND CULTURAL SOCIETY

Fort Mason Center, Building C. (415) 441-0640. Tuesday–Saturday, 12–5. Free.

African and Black American artists and inventors are honored in the exhibit hall of this cultural society. Clothing, pottery, historical documents, and crafts are displayed and a library is open to students of Afro-American history. The exhibit of George Washington Carver's many uses of the peanut is a wonder, as is the one on Black American cowboys.

OCTAGON HOUSE

2645 Gough Street. (415) 885-9796. Second and fourth Thursday and 2nd Sunday of each month, 12–3. Free.

Built in 1861, this unusual eight-sided home is the headquarters of the National Society of the Colonial Dames of America, as well as a gracious museum of Americana. A pack of Revolutionary War playing cards (with soldiers and Indians on the back), a thirteen-star flag, dishes taken in battle by the USS *Constitution* from a British ship during the War of 1812, and a nineteenth-century "mammy bench" make this a pleasantly educational stop.

Nearby Union Street offers blocks of boutiques and restaurants.

MUSEUM OF RUSSIAN CULTURE

2450 Sutter Street. (415) 921-4082. Wednesday and Saturday 12–3, or by appointment. Free.

A visit to this small museum will provide children with a colorful introduction to Russian culture. There are photos, letters, medals, and silks from the families of the Czars—including some funny photos of Anastasia and her sisters. Pushkin and Tolstoy; Pavlova and Nureyev; and other Russian dancers, artists, writers, and scientists are remembered here. The photos and models of Fort Ross are especially noteworthy.

JOSEPHINE D. RANDALL JUNIOR MUSEUM

199 Museum Way off Roosevelt (Upper Market Street area, at Fifteenth Street, west of Castro). (415) 863-1399. Tuesday–Saturday, 10–5. Free.

High on a sunny hill overlooking the city, this museum/zoo is especially designed for children. Here they can watch a seismograph, see dinosaur bones and eggs, learn about the California Indians, and pat a live chicken and pig. They can also talk to crows and mynah birds, handle various minerals and ores, and learn about electricity. During one Saturday visit, youngsters were helping to clean out the cages while two plump raccoons played on the front lawn and Puff the Iguana took an airing on the zookeeper's arm. Members of the Golden Gate Model Railroad Club, located downstairs in the building, allow the public to watch their play with the model trains on the huge room-sized track, on occasional Friday nights.

MISSION DOLORES (MISSION SAN FRANCISCO DE ASIS)

Sixteenth and Dolores. (415) 621-8203. 10–4 in winter, 9–5 in summer. Adults and group tours, $1.

Built in 1776, the mission is San Francisco's oldest structure. The unique Corinthian and Moorish architecture is not at all like other California missions. The cemetery tells many tales.

GOLDEN GATE PARK

From Stanyan Street west to the ocean. The park office is at McLaren Lodge: 588-3706.

There are more than one thousand acres of lakes and greenery in San Francisco's Golden Gate Park and at least one hundred things to see and do.

You can go boating or feed the ducks; cheer toy sailboat races; picnic; ride horses; play tennis, golf or handball; go lawn bowling; watch the grazing buffalo; bicycle; skate; watch soccer and polo matches; pitch horseshoes; shoot arrows; play cards or chess; practice your fly casting; or make water rings in the fountains. Stow Lake is the place to rent rowboats, motor boats, and pedal boats (752-0347). Visit the magical, silvery Golden Gate pavilion from China, located on Stow Lake's island.

The Children's Playground, on the Lincoln Avenue side of the park, features the slide with the fastest ride in the West, plus thirteen other slides, geometrical shapes to climb, and a beautiful carousel, recently restored to its full 1912 glory. There's a small animal farm there, too.

Older children might enjoy a walk through *Shakespeare's Garden* to identify the plants he wrote about, from wormwood and yew to bilberry and eglantine. You can climb a moon bridge in the *Japanese Tea Garden* (Monday–Saturday 9–5; adults 75¢, children 6–12 25¢, San Francisco residents 25¢, free holidays and the first Wednesday of the month), then sit down to tea and cookies in the Japanese Tea House.

Browse through the spun-sugar Victorian *Conservatory* (9–4:30, 558-3973) at any time of year to see displays of flowers in a burgeoning, jungle-like atmosphere. Ring the Mexican Bell in the *Strybing Arboretum's Garden of Fragrance*, where you can also test your powers of smell, touch and taste (8–4:30 weekdays, 10–5 weekends, tours: 558-3623). Gaze at the *Portals of the Past*, the marble columns that are all that was left of a Nob Hill mansion after the Earthquake, and are now the guardians of a duck-filled lake. Don't forget to say thank you to John McLaren (his statute is tucked in a dell of rhododendrons across from the Conservatory—he hated statues in parks) for turning sand dunes into the greenery that graces the City.

M. H. DE YOUNG MEMORIAL MUSEUM

Golden Gate Park, north side of Music Concourse. (415) 221-4811. Wednesday–Sunday 10–5. Adults, $2; ages 12–17 and over 65, 50¢. Free first Wednesday of the month. (One admission charge admits you to the de Young, Asian Art, and the Palace of the Legion of Honor museums on the same day.)

The de Young's romantic Pool of Enchantment, with water lilies and a sculpted boy playing his pipes to two mountain lions, beckons visitors to this land of enchantment. There are paintings, sculpture, tapestries, and graphics by American, Californian, and European artists. The Rembrandts are shown without fanfare and there is a lovely Mary Cassatt in the American section. The American Wing now houses our favorite painting: "Rainy Season in the Tropics" by Frederick Church. Children especially seem to like the "real rooms"—the muraled boudoir from Italy and the Elizabethan paneled bedroom. A pleasant cafeteria is open for lunch and afternoon tea.

ASIAN ART MUSEUM, THE AVERY BRUNDAGE COLLECTION

Golden Gate Park, next to the de Young. (415) 558-2993. 10–5 daily. Same fees and admission arrangements as the de Young.

Chinese galleries on the first floor display objects from prehistoric to nineteenth century, including a magnificent collection of jade in a jewel-box setting: the Magnin jade room. Second floor galleries exhibit art from Japan, Korea, India, Southeast Asia, Tibet, Nepal, and Iran. Both floors overlook the Japanese Tea Garden at the west end, and that museum entrance is used on Mondays and Tuesdays.

CALIFORNIA ACADEMY OF SCIENCE

Golden Gate Park, south side of Music Concourse. (415) 752-8268/4214. Daily 10–5, winter; summer til 7. Adults $2; ages 12–18, $1; ages 6–11, 75¢. Free admission first Wednesday of the month.

Wander through the Hall of North American Mammals, the Hall of Minerals, the Hall of North American Birds (with its model of the Farallon Island bird rookery), or head for the Hall of Fossils to see dinosaur bones, brontosaurus skulls, and a whale skeleton. The Wattis Hall of Man; two African Halls, newly renovated, with sounds of life recorded in Africa; the Hall of Botany; and a new research and space science hall with a shake table that simulates an earthquake lead to the third wing of the Academy.

The Round Bridge in the Japanese Tea Garden

Here you'll find *Morrison Planetarium*, a unique Sky Theater presenting a simulation of the heavens as seen from Earth at any time—past, present, or future—on the sixty-five foot hemispherical dome. Special effects projectors take the viewer through space into whirling galaxies and black holes. Shows change regularly. For daily sky times, call 752-8268. Usually, there are shows at 2 P.M. daily, at 7:30 P.M. on Wednesday and Thursday, and at 12:30, 2, and 3:30 P.M. weekends. Adults, $2, ages 6–17 and seniors, 75¢; under 6 by special permission. "Exploring the Skies of the Season" at 12:30 weekends, 75¢ for all. Closed Thanksgiving and Christmas.

Laserium is a "cosmic" laser show in which colorful images seem to pulsate, float, and dance to the music against a background of stars. Shows ($4.50 for all; 221-0168) are: Friday at 7:30, 9, and 10:30 P.M.; Saturday at 5, 7:30, 9, and 10:30 P.M.; and Sunday at 5, 7:30, and 9 P.M.

The whale fountain courtyard leads to the *Steinhart Aquarium's* swamp, inhabited by crocodiles and alligators. Thousands of fish, reptiles, and dolphins live in 243 colorful tanks, all low enough for children to see into easily. Seahorses; deadly stonefish; dolphins that sound like Flipper; Amazon lettuce-eating manatees; piranhas; and shellfish of all colors, shapes and sizes live here. Upstairs, the *Fish Roundabout* puts you in the middle of a huge tank where fish swim quickly around you. Dolphins are fed every two hours, starting at 10:30 A.M.; the penguins are fed at 11:30 A.M. and 4 P.M. For information, call 752-8268.

THE EXPLORATORIUM

Palace of Fine Arts. Lyon Street. (415) 563-7337. Wednesday–Sunday, 1–5; weekends 11–5; Wednesday, 7–9:30 P.M. Summer hours: Wednesday–Sunday, 11–5. Groups by appointment. Adults, $3, under 17, free.

This is a do-it-yourself museum without walls where visitors are encouraged to see, touch, hear, explore, improvise, and play. Five hundred exhibits feature laser beams, computers, holograms, stereophonic sound testers, radio and TV sets to take apart, and a tactile labyrinth. The Palace of Fine Arts, designed by Bernard Maybeck for the 1915 Exposition, is in one of San Francisco's most romantic spots, with ducks swimming in a beautiful lagoon outside.

PRESIDIO ARMY MUSEUM

Funston and Lincoln Boulevards, Presidio. (415) 561-4115. Tuesday–Sunday, 10–4. Groups by appointment. Free.

Founded by Spain's military forces in 1776, the Presidio has flown Spanish, Mexican, and American flags. Cannons, uniforms, swords, and army memorabilia tell the Presidio's more than two-hundred-year history. Models and carefully wrought dioramas of battlefronts, the 1906 Earthquake, and the 1915 Panama-Pacific Exposition add to the interest of this museum.

Also on the Presidio is the Applied Aquatic Resources Institute (Building 257; Wednesday–Sunday, 1–4, free), an interpretive center demonsrating the wonderment and potential of our aquatic environment.

FORT POINT NATIONAL HISTORIC SITE (GGNRA)

Foot of Marine Drive, under San Francisco end of the Golden Gate Bridge, on the Presidio grounds. (415) 556-1693. Daily 10–5, regular guided tour, and by appointment. Free.

Nestled below the underpinnings of the Golden Gate Bridge, Fort Point, built during the Civil War, is the only brick seacoast fortress in the West—the guardian of San Francisco Bay. With the icy Pacific slamming into the retaining wall and the wind whistling around the point, this is one of the coldest spots in San Francisco. That's why the place was used as a detention barracks and "hardship tour" until World War II. Museum rooms display swords, guns, shells, chains, uniforms, handcuffs, cannon balls, an eyewitness account of the assassination of President Lincoln, relics of the San Francisco earthquake, a Confederate flag, and an old doctor's kit. The gun demonstrations are very popular. And roaming through the dismal jail and barracks and through three floors of echoing hallways, discovering cannons where you least expect them, is the most fun of all.

CALIFORNIA PALACE OF THE LEGION OF HONOR

Lincoln Park, off Thirty-fourth Avenue and Clement. (415) 221-4811. Daily 10–5. Adults, $2; ages 12–17, $1; (Same ticket counts for the Asian Art Museum and the de Young. First of the month is free.)

Children can explore Land's End and get a thrilling view of the Golden Gate Bridge from the ocean side here, after wandering through the impressive marble building and its rotating exhibits and collection of fine French art and twentieth century printmakers. They'll recognize Rodin's "The Thinker" sitting in the courtyard.

THE CLIFF HOUSE (GGNRA)

Land's End. (415) 751-1617. Monday–Friday, 10–4:30; longer hours in summer and on weekends. Free.

"A drive to the 'Cliff' in the early morning . . . and a return to the city through the charming scenery of Golden Gate Park, tends to place man about as near to Elysian bliss as he may hope for in this world." B. E. Lloyd— 1876. A drive to and from the Cliff House can still place you in Elysian bliss, even if the buildings themselves are getting a little ragged around the edges. It's still the best place in town to see the seals on Seal Rocks. There's a shiny new exhibit hall downstairs, showing Cliff House in its various incarnations throughout the years, along with rotating natural history displays under the direction of the National Park Service. Here you can also find out information about Farallon Island tours, the Whale Center (654-6621), and other adventures. And the crammed Musée Mécanique (386-1170; daily, 11–6) houses more than one hundred machines, old and new, which work on small change. Swiss music boxes, a mechanical carnival, a mechanical 1920s farm, old-time movies, and music machines sit alongside Star Trek, electronic games, and modern cartoons. There are restaurants and gift shops upstairs.

SAN FRANCISCO ZOO

Sloat Boulevard and the Great Highway. (415) 661-4844. Daily 10–5. Adults, $2.50; seniors, 50¢; under 15, free. Additional charge for children's zoo, merry-go-round and zoomobile.

Animals from all over the world live here in naturalistic settings. There are cassowary birds and wallaroos, snow leopards, spectacled bears, flamingos, seals, emus, Moulon and Barbary sheep, and peacocks. The main aviary building is a tropical rain forest where you can walk amid 85 species of birds, from pigeons to curassows (11–3 daily). "Creepers," the insect zoo, houses bird-eating spiders, ant lions, tarantulas, and black widows. We always head

California Academy of Science—Moss Photography

for the Big Cat house, where the lions and tigers are fed every day at 2 (except Monday, because in the jungle they don't eat every day). And the animals in the barnyard are there to be petted. The zoo is right near the ocean, so it's wise to have sweaters handy. New exhibits include Gorilla World, Wolf Woods, Musk Ox Meadow, the African Scene, the Tuxedo Junction Penguin Pool, and the Primate Discovery Center, 5 stories of open atriums, wild meadows, pools, a night gallery, and hands-on learning exhibits.

CROSSROADS FARM

1499 Potrero Avenue, at Army Street freeway exit. (415) 826-4290, Daily 9–5. Free.
This community center for theater and environmental arts offers garden tours and feeding and milking and egg-collecting experiences for young farmers. The community gardens planted by children and adults are there to bring people together.

PUBLIC RELATIONS TOURS

KSFO AND KYA *300 Broadway. (415) 398-5600. Free, by appointment.* See news production, the music library, traffic continuity and disc jockeys in action.

MARIN COUNTY

Marin County is a land of mountains and seashore, north of Golden Gate Bridge. Most of the "places" to go with children in Marin are natural wonders. You can drive to the top of Mt. Tamalpais and walk the trails overlooking miles of ocean, land, and city. You can explore the silent redwood groves of Muir Woods, then travel on to Stinson or one of the lesser known beaches for a seaside picnic, rock-hunting and driftwood-collecting, or even a quick dip in the icy sea. You can also spend hours fishing in the Marin lakes, or hiking the beautiful Point Reyes National Seashore area. And when you feel the need for civilization, you can head for Tiburon or Sausalito, where the children will be as enchanted as you by the appearance and attractions of these bayside villages.

SAUSALITO

After stopping for a moment to look back at the Golden Gate Bridge from Vista Point, or after taking the short drive to the California Marine Mammal Center at the Marin Headlands Ranger Station in Fort Cronkhite (331-SEAL; daily, 10–4) to see seals being cared for until they can return to their natural environment, spend a few hours in the Riviera by the Bay. Noted for years as an artist's colony, the village of Sausalito is now a mecca for tourists and young people. There are clothing and toy stores, ice cream parlors and coffee houses, art galleries and restaurants for every age, taste, and budget. Visitors can climb up the stairs from Bridgeway to The Alta Mira (126 Harrison Avenue, 332-1350; 8 A.M.–9 P.M.) for an elegant brunch and a breathtaking view of San Francisco or head for lunch right on the water. The Sausalito Historical Museum, in the old City Hall on Litho Street (Wednesday and Saturday 1–5, Sunday 10–5; 332-1005) offers police and railroad memorabilia, period costumes, and photos of the town since 1860. My nephew's favorite pastime however, is simply walking along the rocks and finding baby crabs. The Marin Headlands ranger station (561-7612), the Mt. Tamalpais State Parks (388-2070), and Muir and Stinson Beach ranger stations (868-0942, 868-1922) can give you up-to-the-minute weather information before you set out.

SAN FRANCISCO BAY–DELTA MODEL

2100 Bridgeway, Sausalito. (415) 332-3870. Tuesday–Saturday, 9–4, and by appointment. Free.

The U.S. Army Corps of Engineers has put together a hydraulic scale model of San Francisco Bay and the Sacramento–San Joaquin Delta. The model shows the action of the tides, the flow and currents of the water, and the mixing of sea water and fresh water. Guided tours take one-and-one-half hours, but individuals can use the self-guided recorded tour system to see the exhibit at their own speed. A multimedia program presenting a history of the bay is in the works. It's a good idea to call first—the model is not always in action.

TIBURON

Named *Punta de Tiburon*, or Shark Point, by early Spanish settlers, Tiburon is a quiet, one-street bayside village, a nice place to spend a sunny afternoon. Lunch and a drink while enjoying the view from one of the many restaurants on the bay can be heaven. Nautical shops, a Swedish bakery, and the bookstore are all fun to browse through. Hardy walkers can head up the hill to the Landmark Society Museum in Old St. Hilary's Church (Sunday and Wednesday, 1–4, April–September and by appointment; (415) 435-1853; 50¢) to see a changing art exhibit and specimens of the local plants that grow nowhere else in the world. On the way back to Highway 101 stop at the Richardson wildlife sanctuary (376 Greenwich Beach Road; 388-2524). Youngsters can explore the sea life and observe birds along self-guided natural trails in the sanctuary, open Wednesday–Sunday 9–5, 50¢. There are special programs and films on Sundays.

ANGEL ISLAND STATE PARK

In San Francisco Bay. (415) 435-1915. For tour information: 546-2852. For ferry information from San Francisco see San Francisco chapter. Ferries leave from Tiburon daily in summer, weekends in winter. Adults, $6; children, $3.25. Prices include park fee.

Secluded picnic groves, beaches, forest trails, and historic military buildings under reconstruction make Angel Island a wonderful place to spend the day. An elephant train jaunts around the island (adults, $1.50; children, 75¢) to give you a good picture of these 740 acres, discovered in 1775 by Juan Manuel de Ayala. The deer are surprisingly brash.

MUIR WOODS NATIONAL MONUMENT

Off Highway 1, on Muir Woods Road. (415) 388-2595. Daily, 8 A.M.–sunset. Free.

This lovely forest of giant coast redwoods, some more than two hundred feet high, is a breathtaking way to start the day. Among these magnificent trees, you'll encounter many other species of plant life—azalea, red alder, and California laurels—as well as an occasional black-tailed deer scampering across the trail and, in summer, young salmon and trout swimming through Redwood Creek. Although the main inner trail of the forest is paved, the outer trails are natural earth for easy walking. A self-guiding natural trail along the creek helps you understnd the forest. A lunch counter, gift shop and ranger's station are located near the park entrance.

MARIN COUNTY HISTORICAL SOCIETY MUSEUM

1125 B Street, Boyd Park, San Rafael. (415) 454-8538. Wednesday–Saturday 1–4 P.M. Free.

Designed "to stir the imagination and bring back panoramas of the past" this overstuffed, cheerful museum displays original Mexican land grants and mementos of the Miwoks, Mexicans, and pioneers who settled Marin. Lillie Coit's shoes, Mrs. Berryessa's silk shawl, an early San Quentin oil lamp, and the military collection are fascinating. Our youngsters' favorite thing was the huge tallow kettle at the entrance. Once used for boiling elk tallow at the Rancho Olompali, the kettle was also used as a stewpot for the military during the Bear Flag War. Today it's a great hiding place.

Just down the block is the *Mission San Rafael Archangel* (1104 Fifth Avenue, (415) 454-8141; 11–4 daily, except Sunday, 10–4. Free). A small display of mission furniture and Spanish tapestries is in the gift shop, photos and arrowheads and priests' garments are displayed in windows outside, and the small chapel flies the six flags under which the mission has served: Spain, Mexico, the California Republic, the United States of 1850, the Vatican, and the United States of America.

A few blocks across town, the *Marin Wildlife Center* (76 Albert Park Lane; (415) 454-6961; Tuesday–Saturday, 10–4; donations) is a small wildlife rehabilitation and nature education center. The animals on exhibit, such as a bear, birds, raccoon, owls, and a hawk can never be released because they can no longer fend for themselves in the wilds. Dioramas of Marin County's forest, salt marsh, chaparral, seashore, and grasslands exhibit the animals of the area.

AUDUBON CANYON RANCH

Highway 1, 3 miles north of Stinson Beach. (415) 383-1644. Saturday, Sunday and holidays, 10–4, March 1–July 4; and by appointment. Free.

This one-thousand-acre wildlife sanctuary bordering on the Bolinas Lagoon is a peaceful spot to view birds "at home." From a hilltop, you can watch the nesting activities of the great blue heron and great egret. The ranch's pond, stream, and canyon are a living demonstration of the region's ecology—the delicate balance between plant and animal life and their environment. The display hall shows local fauna and flora and information on the San Andreas fault. Picnic areas are available.

The Birds come to a Marin picnic

POINT REYES NATIONAL SEASHORE

Highway 1, Olema. (415) 663-1092. 8 A.M. to sundown daily. Free.

Sir Francis Drake is said to have landed here in 1579. The beauty of the sharp cliffs, swimmable and unswimmable surf, streams, tidepools, lowlands, and forest meadows makes you wonder why he went back to England. You can watch the bird rookeries in the trees and sea lion rocks offshore. You can walk along well-marked nature trails, including an earthquake trail; hike; backpack; and camp. The information center at Olema has a natural history exhibit and the Park Service raises Morgan horses nearby. We like Drake's Beach best and before we set out, we call the ranger's office there (669-1250) to make sure it's sunny.

The Point Reyes Lighthouse is now open to the public, 10–5 Thursday–Monday, weather permitting (669-1534).

A new part of Point Reyes is *Kule Loklo,* the Miwok Village. Visitors can see a reconstructed sweat house and huts built with the original materials as well as artifacts such as hunting snares and sewing implements. There are skills demonstrations on Saturday and Sunday 9 to 3.

Tomales Bay State Park (8–8 in summer, 8–6 in winter daily; 669-1140; $1 per car) is part of the Point Reyes National Seashore, too. Craggy Bishop pines, sandy beaches, and tidepools are the attractions here. Tidepools are the rocky pockets that retain seawater when the tide goes out. Many strange animals and plants live among their rocks—seaweeds, anemones, barnacles, worms, jellyfish, shellfish, sand dollars, urchins, tiny fish, and algae. The best way to look at a tidepool is to lie very quietly until the tidepool's occupants think you're part of the landscape and continue to move through their daily paces. Tidepool animals may not be collected, but their activity will provide many engrossing on-the-spot hours for children and adults as well.

MARIN FRENCH CHEESE COMPANY

7500 Red Hill Road, Petaluma (9 miles west of Novato on Novato Boulevard). (415) 762-6001. Sales room, with tasting and tour, 10–4 daily. Free.

Situated next to a pond in the rolling, cow-speckled hills between Novato and the coast, this is a perfect destination for an afternoon outing or picnic. A 15-minute tour begins with the 4,000 gallon tank of milk and takes you through the different stages of cheese making—heating the milk, adding the three "cheese" ingredients (culture, enzymes, and starter), and aging. You pass shiny steel tubes and tanks and different aging rooms, each with its own smell. Picnic tables are available, where you can sit and eat a picnic lunch made from ingredients available in the store.

MARIN MUSEUM OF THE AMERICAN INDIAN

2200 Novato Boulevard, Miwok Park, Novato. (415) 897-4064. Tuesday–Saturday 10–4; Sunday 12–4. Free.

Exhibits and a diorama illustrate the prehistoric period in Marin County. Coast Miwoks are represented by decorated baskets, cooking implements, and stone tools. Changing exhibits interpret other Native American cultures. Classes, lectures, and films are given, so call for schedules. The California Native Plant Garden and surrounding park are suitable for nature walks and picnics.

NAPA, SONOMA, AND LAKE COUNTIES

Napa, Sonoma, and Lake counties are best known for the vineyards that grow on rolling hills and in the Valley of the Moon. Wineries can be fun for children to visit, not only because the wine-making process is fascinating but because the wine industry is part of California's history and culture. In most wineries, your tour will follow the direction the grape takes, from delivery from the vineyards, to the crushing, to the aging vat, to the bottles in the tasting rooms. The listed wineries offer the most interesting plants and tours, all of which are free (including the "tasting" for the older folks). But the country itself is welcoming and seen best from the hot air balloons, gliders, planes, and parachutes now available for the brave of heart.

YOUNTVILLE-VINTAGE 1870

Highway 29, Yountville (707) 944-2788. Daily, 10 5.
 This lovely old former winery is part of the original land grant made to Salvador Vallejo in 1838 and was bought in 1870 for $250 in U.S. gold coin. The brick exterior of the building hasn't changed much, but the interior is now a charming complex of shops, theaters, candle and candy makers, potters, a glass blower, and a leather craftsman, who work in open stores. The Vintage Railroad specialty shops are housed in nine authentically restored railroad cars, including two cabooses.

DOMAINE CHANDON

2280 California Drive, Yountville, (707) 944-8844. Restaurant reservations; 944-2467. 10–4:30 except Monday and Tuesday.
 This star in the winery chain on Highway 29 makes sparkling wine that's rosy-gold and golden pink. The tour takes you past James Bond-ian huge vats and into musty cellars where each bottle must be turned every day. The restaurant is French and very classy and the grounds, with streams and ponds, are welcoming.

ROBERT MONDAVI WINERY

Highway 29, Oakville, (707) 963-9611. Daily, 10:30–4:30. Free.
Designed and landscaped by Cliff May, who designed the Sunset Magazine building, the Mondavi Winery offers jazz concerts and special events on summer Sundays on the center lawn.

NAPA VALLEY OLIVE OIL MANUFACTORY

End of Charter Oak Road, St. Helena, (707) 963-4173. Daily, 8–6.
A visit to the wineries is not complete without a stop at this old-fashioned olive oil factory and sausage and cheese store. Hidden at the end of a block on the southern entrance to town, the place looks more like a deserted barn than a bustling business. Inside you'll find vast amounts of cheese, glistening pyramids of olive oil bottles, sausages, and stacks of Italian delicacies. Picnic tables are available.

THE SILVERADO MUSEUM

1490 Library Avenue, St. Helena. (707) 963-3757. Daily, 12–4, except Monday and holidays. Free.
Robert Louis Stevenson has been associated with the Napa Valley ever since he spent a honeymoon in an abandoned bunkhouse of the Silverado Mine on Mount St. Helena. Today, anyone who grew up on *A Child's Garden of Verses* or *Treasure Island* will appreciate this tribute to the man who wrote them. Portraits of Stevenson abound, including one showing him as a young boy with long flowing curls. Original manuscripts, illustrations, the author's toy lead soldiers, his tea set, doll, chess set and cigarette holder, Henry James's gloves, and memorabilia from the plantation in Samoa are neatly displayed in this cheerful museum.

CHRISTIAN BROTHERS WINERY

Highway 29, St. Helena. (707) 963-2719. Daily, 10–4:30. Free.
This imposing castle, the largest stone winery in the world, is the center for the good Brothers' wine aging and champagne cellar. Brother Timothy's corkscrew collection is on view in the display area.

FREEMARK ABBEY

Highway 29, St. Helena. (707) 963-7211. Winery open 10–4:30 daily, tours at 2 P.M.; shops open 10–5:30. Free.
The old Freemark Abbey Winery now houses the Hurd Beeswax Candle Factory, a small winery and gift shop, with adjoining coffee shop, restaurant, and delicatessen. Weekday visitors may see the candlemakers working until 4:30. On the far wall of the inside showroom, a wooden shutter opens to reveal the back of a beehive full of bees filling their honeycomb.

THE OLD BALE MILL

Highway 29, St. Helena. Daily, 10–4:30. Free.

Dr. E. T. Bale built this gristmill in 1846 and the last flour was ground here in 1879. One hundred years later, the state is restoring the mill and will soon be selling mill-ground flour to visitors who'll enjoy seeing the mill in action.

STERLING VINEYARDS

1111 Dunaweal Lane, off Highway 29, Calistoga. (707) 942-5151. 10:30–4:30, except Monday and Tuesday in winter. $3 per person.

An aerial tramway takes visitors high into the hills to see galleries and unusual exhibits in the winery. The ride is three minutes of excitement; there can be a long wait.

Sterling Vineyards aerial tramway

SHARPSTEEN MUSEUM AND SAM BRANNAN COTTAGE

1311 Washington Street, Calistoga. (707) 942-5911. May 1–November 2, 10–4 daily; December 1–April 1, 12–4. Free.

Calistoga's romantic pioneer history comes alive in the scale model dioramas and shadow boxes. A model of Calistoga in 1865 covers one wall, others show Robert Louis Stevenson and his wife, the railroad depot (with model train) and China Camp complex, and the toll house. One of Sam Brannan's cottages (he was California's first millionaire, but died broke) has been moved to the site and refurbished right down to the ivory dressing set on the dresser. A big C&C Stage Line stagecoach stands near the front door along with a collection of hubcaps from the era of wooden spokes and gas lamps from early cars. Local artist Ben Sharpsteen donated his money, time, and talent in creating this wonderful museum.

OLD FAITHFUL GEYSER OF CALIFORNIA

1299 Tubbs Lane, Calistoga. (707) 942-6463. Daily, 9–6 summer, 9–5 winter. Adults, $2; ages 6–12, $1. Tour discounts. Picnic area.

One of the three faithful geysers in the world, this one erupts 350-degree water about every forty minutes to heights of about 60 feet. The geyser rumbles, belches forth a small fountain, rumbles for about three more minutes, then gushes forth a rainbow of foaming steam and water. A tape gives historical and geological information and tells how geysers are formed. The owners use another geyser on the property to heat their house, and there is a wishing well nearby with 130-degree water.

THE PETRIFIED FOREST

Petrified Forest Road, between Calistoga and Santa Rosa. (707) 942-6667. Daily, 9–5; open in summer until 6. Over age 10, $3.

Volcanic eruptions of Mount St. Helena six million years ago formed this forest of petrified redwoods, discovered in 1870 and written about by Robert Louis Stevenson. A lovely forest trail passes a three hundred-foot-long "Monarch" tunnel tree and "the Giant" that was already 3,000 years old when it was buried. On the way out, you'll walk through a specimen shop of fossils and petrified worms, snails, clams, nuts, and wood.

AIR PLAY

The rolling hills and soft wind currents of the area have made the skies here especially accessible. For those who are adventurous, try the following:

HOT AIR BALLOON RIDES

Great Pacific Hot Air Balloon Co., P. O. Box 656 Napa, 94558 (707) 224-4173.

Adventures Aloft, 6525 Washington Street, Yountville 94599 (707) 255-8688.

AeroStat Renaissance and Ballooning Co., 1644 Silverado Trail, Napa 94558 (707) 255-6356.

Airborn of Sonoma Co., P.O. Box 789, Sebastopol 95472 (707) 823-8757.

GLIDER RIDES

Calistoga Soaring Center, 1546 Lincoln Avenue, Calistoga 94515 (707) 942-5592.

OLD UNCLE GAYLORD'S

824 Petaluma Boulevard, South Petaluma. (707) 778-6008. Groups by appointment. Free. The 30-minute tour shows the methods and equipment used to make ice cream the old way, with rock salt and ice. There's an ice cream museum and complementary ice cream comes right out of the maker.

PETALUMA ADOBE

3325 Adobe Road, Petaluma (east of Highway 101). (707) 762-4871. Daily, 10–5. Tickets usable at all state parks that day; adults, 50¢; children, 25¢.

General Mariano G. Vallejo's ranch house, Rancho Petaluma, was built in 1836 as the centerpiece of a Mexican land grant of 66,600 acres. Here we learned that in Spanish adobe means *to mix,* and that the thick, naturally insulating bricks were made from clay mixed with water and straw and then dried in the sun. Visitors walk through the adobe on a self-guided tour. The kitchen, workshop, candle room, weaving room, servants' quarters, and the Vallejos' living quarters upstairs are graciously furnished with some of the original pieces. Outside, there are huge iron cauldrons, clay ovens, a covered wagon, and the racks on which hides—a currency of the period—were stretched out to dry. At one time, General Vallejo had one thousand workers on the ranch, and it's not hard, standing before Rancho Petaluma today, to imagine the bustle of yesteryear.

DEPOT MUSEUM

Depot Park, between First Street E and First Street W., Sonoma. (707) 938-9765. Wednesday–Sunday, 1–4:30. Adults, 50¢; children, 25¢. Free school tours by appointment.

The restored North West Pacific Railroad Station now houses a spiffy new historical museum and pioneer exhibit. The old Union Hall theater curtain, filled with ads, forms one wall. The old station master's office is now a reference library. A Victorian living room, dining room, and kitchen has been created and there are grizzly bear feet, saddles, sewing machines, and an exhibit of the Native American local tribes. A boxcar, cattlecar, and gazebo are being put in order for public use. Picnic facilities are nearby, as are bocceball courts.

SONOMA STATE HISTORICAL PARK

From Third Street West and down West Spain Street past the Sonoma Plaza to Third

Street East. (707) 938-4779. Daily, 10–5. Tickets usable at all state parks that day; adults, 50¢; children, 25¢.

Lachryma Montis, at Third Street West, named after the clear spring, "Tear of the Mountain," was General Vallejo's city house. Furnished precisely as it was when he lived there with his family, right down to the photograph of Abraham Lincoln on the wall, the house feels as if Vallejo just stepped out for a moment. One daughter's painting is on a wall, along with family photos. Behind the house is the kitchen building and the Chinese cook's quarters. The Chalet in front was once the storehouse and is now a Vallejo museum containing his books, pictures, saddles, coach and cattle brand, various remembrances of his family, and biographies of ten of his sixteen children.

On the Plaza, you'll walk by Vallejo's first home in Sonoma. Destroyed by a fire in 1867, only the Indian servants' wing survives. You can walk through it and see a small Indian exhibit in the ranger's building. Next, *The Toscano Hotel*, built in 1858, is a carefully restored mining hotel with Scott Joplin music playing in the lobby and the cards and whiskey glasses still on the tables from the century-ago players. (Tours are 10–5 daily in summer, 11–1 on Tuesday, and 1–4 weekends in winter.)

The Mission San Francisco Solano was the most northern and last built of the twenty-one Franciscan missions in California and the only one established under Mexican rule (1823). The padres' quarters is the oldest structure in Sonoma. Visitors can walk through the building, looking at mission exhibits, furnished rooms of the padres, spurs and leggings of the *vaqueros*, and other interesting artifacts of mission life, including a primitively painted chapel. A *ramada* is being constructed in the garden for blacksmith, weaving, breadbaking, and other period crafts demonstrations.

Blue Wing Inn, across the street, was once a hotel visited by John Fremont; Kit Carson; generals Grant, Sherman, and P. Smith; and the bandit Joaquin Murietta. At present it is a complex of shops, but the state is restoring it to its former glory. The *Sonoma Barracks* is now a history museum.

During your wanderings you may want to stop in at the *Sonoma Cheese Factory* (2 Spain Street, (707) 938-5225, 9–6 daily) to see a slide show, young men pounding cheese bags to make Sonoma Jack, and to pick up a picnic— which you can then enjoy in the Sonoma Plaza behind City Hall and the Bear Flag Monument honoring the short-lived Bear Flag Republic. There are two fine slides in the town square playground.

BUENA VISTA WINERY

1 mile out on East Napa Road, Sonoma. (707) 938-8504. Daily, 10–5. Free.

Buena Vista was the first winery with stone cellars in California. Founded in 1857 by the Hungarian count, Agoston Haraszthy, who first imported European grape varieties for commercial use, Buena Vista winery is now a California historical landmark. The self-guided tour in leaking limestone caves is wonderfully atmospheric. There are picnic tables and the children's playground is made of casks and barrels.

SEBASTIANI VINEYARDS

389 East Fourth Street, Sonoma. (707) 938-5532. Daily, 10–5. Free.

Commemorated as one of the oldest vineyards in Northern California, Sebastiani is known for the carved oak casks and redwood tanks. Founded in 1825, this third generation winery began with a five hundred gallon tank and primitive equipment. There's a small Native American exhibit on the grounds.

The miniature railroad at Traintown

TRAINTOWN

Broadway, Sonoma. (707) 938-3912. Daily, 10:30–5:30 in summer and winter weekends. Adults, $2; children, $1.25.

A fifteen-minute trip on the Sonoma Steam Railroad, a quarter-size reproduction of a mountain division steam railroad of the 1890s, takes you over trestles, past trees, lakes, tunnels and bridges, and into Traintown. While the train takes on water in Lakeview, you can look at this quarter-sized miniature mining town, while listening to its recorded history and feeling like Gulliver in the land of Lilliputians.

JACK LONDON STATE HISTORIC PARK

Glen Ellen. (707) 938-5216. Daily, 10–5. $2 per car for the museum and the newly enlarged park.

Charmian London built the House of Happy Walls as a memorial to her husband. Furnished with the furniture and art gathered for Wolf House, which burned before the Londons could move into it, this museum thoroughly covers the life of the adventurous young man. Once a sailor, prospector, and roustabout, London struggled to gain acceptance as a writer—and you can see a collection of his rejection slips. Photos of the *Snark*, in which the Londons sailed the South Pacific, and treasures collected on their voyages line the walls. Books sold by the ranger are stamped with London's signature (the stamp he used to save time). London was also an experimental farmer and thirty-nine acres of his Beauty Ranch have just been purchased by the state. Here you'll see the cottage where he did his writing, concrete silos, the distillery, stallion barn, log bathhouse, and blacksmith's shop. A trail still leads to the Wolf House ruins and to London's grave. Picnic areas are available.

THE WORLD OF JACK LONDON

Jack London Village, 14300 Arnold Drive, Glen Ellen. (707) 996-2888. Wednesday–Sunday 10–6 (but there are always books on sale on the honor system outside the store.)

Located in a marvelous bookshop specializing in books by Jack London and his friends, this unique museum is a collection of posters made for movies of Jack London's books, plaques, pictures, dishes, memorial cups, letters to and from fans, old checks, Charmian London's typewriter, first editions, scrapbooks, and remembrances. Even the guest book makes good reading!

SONOMA COUNTY FARM TRAILS

P.O. Box 6674, Santa Rosa, CA 95406. For a copy of the map send stamped, self-addressed envelope.

Drive from a mushroom farm and eggery in Petaluma to apple farms in Sebastopol, turkey growers, or Christmas tree farms. The map lists Farm Trail members and has a handy product reference guide. California Christmas Tree Growers are listed at 2855 Telegraph Avenue, Berkeley, CA 94705.

SONOMA COUNTY HISTORICAL MUSEUM

557 Summerfield Road, Santa Rosa. (707) 539-0556. Daily, 1–5 except Monday. Free.

Old photos of the county and of San Francisco before and after 1906, a 1902 Sears Roebuck catalog, the Delft plate sent by the Dutch in 1947 as thanks to Santa Rosa's children for three thousand pounds of clothing donated in a war-relief drive, and the first Santa Rosa entry (1966) to the Soap Box Derby are among the many items in this fine collection (scheduled to move to new quarters in the next few months). The nearby Codding Museum of Natural History (1–5 Saturday and Sunday, free) shows dioramas of big game in their native habitat.

RIPLEY'S BELIEVE IT OR NOT MEMORIAL MUSEUM

492 Sonoma Avenue, Juilliard Park; Santa Rosa Avenue, Santa Rosa. (707) 528-5233. Daily 11–4 in summer; Thursday–Monday September 1–December 15 and February 16–May 15. Adults, 50¢; under 12, 10¢.

Nestled in tall redwoods, this little church, built from *one* tree, houses personal articles and drawings of the Believe-It-or-Not man. A wax figure of Ripley looks out at photos of him with Will Rogers and Shirley Temple, and newspaper clippings as well as samplings of the curiosities he'd collected. You might hear some of the "Believe It or Not" radio shows if the guard has time to play them for you.

Across the street is the Luther Burbank Memorial Garden with a kiosk telling the story of his life and showing some of his tools. Burbank's Home at Santa Rosa and Sonoma Avenues, is now open Tuesday to Sunday for tours 12–3:30: (707) 539-3428. Adults, $1; and by appointment, 576-5115. Paderewski played on the piano downstairs; the piano shawl was a gift from Queen Victoria.

JESSE PETER MEMORIAL MUSEUM

Santa Rosa Junior College. 1501 Mendocino Avenue, Santa Rosa. (707) 527-4179. 12–4 weekdays and by appointment. Free. Visitor parking behind Bailey Field.

Native American arts are prized in this bustling tiny center. Pottery, drums, crafts, sculpture, a Tule balsa canoe, jars, slide show, and grinding stones are all part of a changing exhibit.

EDWIN LANGHART HEALDSBURG MUSEUM

133 Matheson Street, Healdsburg. (707) 433-4717. Tuesday–Saturday, 12–5. Free.

Treasures from the collections of local families have formed the nucleus of this fine outgrowth of our Bicentennial. Dolls, sewing machines, books, toys, gentlemen's accessories and ladies' clothing, a 1904 washer, an 1892 people-drawn fire engine, a cradle scythe, a funny carved wooden rooster, false teeth, and pictures of the geysers are part of this growing display.

CANOE TRIPS ON THE RUSSIAN RIVER

W. C. "Bob" Trowbridge, 20 Healdsburg Avenue, Healdsburg, CA 95448. (707) 433-7247.Twenty-eight dollars per canoe. Over 5 years of age only. Reservations advised. For information on trips on the American River, Sacramento River, and Colorado River, call or write.

The picturesque, winding Russian River is perfect for family canoe trips. It's safe and lovely but can also be fast enough to be exciting. One-, two-, and half-day trips are available and there's chicken barbeque on weekends in summer. Swimmers only!

ITALIAN SWISS COLONY WINERY

Highway 101, Asti. (707) 894-2541. Daily 10–5. Free.
    Scientists will enjoy seeing stainless steel tanks, shining pipes, and chemistry laboratories. Picnic facilities are available.

UNION HOTEL RESTAURANT

Occidental. (707) 874-3662. Lunch on weekdays, $4; dinner nightly, 2–9; Sundays and holidays 12–8; $5.95–$11.25.
    Dining at the Union Hotel, which has been in business since 1867, is more than just a meal, it's an experience: Italian food served family-style on a plastic red-checked tablecloth with more food than you can possibly eat. One lunch consisted of salami and cheese, bean vinaigrette, salad, clam chowder, chicken, zucchini fritters, bread and butter, and pasta. Chicken, duck, and steak are the evening choices—with salami and cheese, bean salad, thick soup, pickled salad, green salad, sourdough bread and sweet butter,

Fort Ross Chapel

pasta, vegetables, potatoes, side dishes—and dessert. Paper bags for "tomorrow's lunch" come with the check. Everything tastes delicious—especially if you've primed yourself by starving for awhile beforehand.

DUNCAN MILLS DEPOT MUSEUM

Highway 116/Moscow Road, 4 miles from the ocean, Duncan Mills. (707) 865-2573. Saturday 10–3. Free.

The only remaining depot of the North Pacific Coast Railroad, which ran the Sausalito-Cazadero route from 1877 to 1935, is now a small museum of railroad history and the reception office for Duncan Mills Campground. Tools, telegraph keys, bottles, photos, books, and various vestiges of the logging railway may be seen. Duncan Mills is a growing outpost, with leather; cheese; and book, jewelry, and food stores springing up in Victorian style.

FORT ROSS STATE HISTORIC PARK

Highway 1, 12 miles north of Jenner. (707) 847-3286. Daily 10–4:30; $2 per car. Guided tours Sunday afternoons and by appointment. Free audio wands (including Russian language) for self-guided tours.

Fifty-nine buildings, nine of which are inside the redwood walls of the fort, are being rebuilt in a major state restoration project. The Russian Chapel, with a ringable bell in front, is as spare and quiet as it was when the fort was sold to John Sutter in 1841. Visitors can climb up into the eight-sided blockade tower and seven-sided blockade to look out over the little beach and inlet where Russian fur merchants used to trade with the Indians. The Commodore's house serves as a small museum, with a Russian samovar, tools, native plant exhibits, an Aleut kayak, and artifacts found on the grounds. The puppet story of Princess Helene Gagarin's abduction by Chief Solano and her subsequent rescue by General Vallejo, Solano's blood brother, is a romantic fantasy loosely based on fact. Don't forget to toss a wish into the wishing well!

LAKE COUNTY MUSEUM

Old Courthouse, Main Street, Lakeport. (707) 263-4555. Wednesday–Saturday, 10–4 in winter, also Sunday in summer.

Photos of yesteryear—the old spas and steamships—are favorites in this pioneer and Native American collection. An old·musket used in the Revolutionary War, a barbed wire collection, a gem collection (Lake County is known for its "moon tears," or semiprecious diamonds), clocks, and clothes are here, along with Pomo baskets, feather polychrome baskets, a Tule boat, a rare rabbit blanket, and arrowheads.

REDWOOD COUNTRY: MENDOCINO, HUMBOLDT, AND DEL NORTE COUNTIES

Redwood Country is one of the most beautiful areas in America. Stately redwoods line the roads "as far as the fog flows" and the Pacific Ocean crashes into the shoreline. Some of the beaches are craggy and surrounded by dangerous currents. Others are calm and protected, with long empty stretches just made for solitary walks. You can dash up from San Francisco on Highway 101 or you can spend hours wending along the coastline on Highway 1. You can enjoy the Victoriana of Ferndale and Eureka or you can lose yourself in the tiny fishing villages of Rockport and Noyo. Whale watching is a popular pastime from December to April. The waters may be too cold to swim in, but the fish thrive and are there for the catching. You can get away from it all in the sylvan glens and picnic areas along the Avenue of the Giants, marveling on man's smallness next to a three hundred foot tree. Redwood Country lets you set your own pace—there are many places to see and things to do close to each other, and there are enough parks and beaches for you to relax or picnic in, whenever the mood strikes. It's a perfect place for a weekend, or a week.

MENDOCINO

Once an old lumber port, settled in 1852, Mendocino is now a mecca for driftwood collectors and artists. The town has appeared in many movies and there are interesting little streets to browse along when it gets too foggy for beachcombing. Among the highlights in town are The Mendocino Art Center (540 Little Lake Street. 10–5 daily; special movies and shows at night; (707) 937-5819); The Mendocino Ice Cream Company on Main (937-5844); Sky's No Limit, the kite and frisbee store on Main (937-0173) and Kolorphorme, the toy store for all ages down the block (937-0100). The old Masonic Lodge Hall, at Lansing and Ukiah, with its massive redwood sculpture of Father Time And The Maiden, carved from one piece of redwood, is a landmark, and the Kelly House Historical Museum, on Main, is currently being restored (957-5791; Friday–Tuesday and by appointment; free) to its 1861 state and will be a memory-filled museum.

MASONITE CORPORATION DEMONSTRATION FOREST

Highway 128 between Navarro and Little River.

This six hundred-yard forest trail shows a commercially grown forest. Points of interest are well-marked. A display of how masonite is made from log leftovers, to chips, to fiber, to blank board, to pressed board, to panels and finally used is available, as is a nice picnic area.

GEORGIA PACIFIC LOGGING MUSEUM

Main Street, Fort Bragg. (707) 964-5651. Wednesday–Sunday, 8:30–4:30. Free.

A huge slice of redwood that was 1,753 years old in 1843 is on display along with logging machinery. Inside, historical pictures of the industry, huge bellows, mementos of the loggers, and ship's models complete the museum collection, diagonally across from the Skunk Depot. Occasional films help accentuate the differences between the smooth industrial present and the rugged past in logging. Nearby, at the foot of Walnut Street, is the Georgia Pacific Nursery (9–4 weekdays, April–November) which holds four million trees. A display room explains reforestation and timber management. An arboretum, nature trails, and picnic tables are available. A free packet of redwood seeds is mailed to each visiting family.

MENDOCINO COAST BOTANICAL GARDENS

18220 North Highway 1, 2 miles south of Fort Bragg. (707) 964-4352. Adults, $4; ages 12–17 and seniors, $1.50. Daily 9–6 in summer; weekends, weather permitting, in winter.

Whole families of quail live in this flower-laden, 47-acre forest and sea coast garden. Visitors walk through nurseries, beside twinkling brooks, over wooden bridges, and out to the very edge of the ocean. A cliffhouse overlooks the sea-swept rocks. Picnic areas are available, as is a nursery.

THE SKUNK RAILROAD

Skunk Depot, Fort Bragg. (707) 964-6371. Reservations advised, write California Western Railroad, P.O. Box 907, Fort Bragg 95437. Half- and full-day trips from and to Fort Bragg and Willits to Northspur are available at prices ranging from about $5 for children for a 3-hour trip to about $12 for adults for the full day.

The Skunk Railroad, named for the smell the first gas engines used to cast over the countryside, has been making passenger trips from Fort Bragg to Willits since 1911. During the forty-mile trip the train crosses thirty-two trestles and bridges, goes through two tunnels, twists and turns over spectacularly curved track, and travels from the quiet Noyo riverbed to high mountain passes through redwood forest. The bouncy diesel Skunk is well worth the price and time. One train even has an open observation car.

WELLER HOUSE

524 Stewart, Fort Bragg (707) 964-3061, 10–5 p.m. Tuesday–Saturday in summer. Donation.

This private home is on the National Register of Historic Places because of the outstanding use of redwood, especially in the breathtaking 3rd floor ballroom. Children may look through a stereoscope, listen to a 1912 harpsichord and a crank gramophone, view ship models, push a 1929 toy train, touch marble and horsehair furniture and even visit the owner's grandmother's antique doll.

The *Fort Bragg Fort* nearby on Franklin Street is also of interest to youngsters.

MENDOCINO COUNTY MUSEUM

400 East Commercial Street, Willits. (707) 459-2736. 10–4:30, Wednesday–Sunday. Ages 19–64, 75¢; 11–18, 50¢; 65 and over, 25¢.

The Skunk Railroad

Historical articles and documents reflecting Mendocino County's past have been gathered for this interesting collection that includes a peddler's wagon, stagecoaches, a lumber room, restored kitchen, living and bedrooms, Pomo baskets, and a wonderful assortment of hats. If the Skunk Railroad leaves you in Willits with time to spend, this museum is a nice way to do it.

THE DRIVE-THRU TREE

Old Highway 101, Leggett. (707) 925-6363. Daily, 9–6, later in summer. $2 per car.

This large, chandelier-shaped, 315-foot redwood was tunneled in 1934 and a standard-size contemporary car just fits through. It's twenty-one feet in diameter and—in spite of the tunnel—is still alive. The winding dirt road leading to the tree takes you right to a little gift shop and on to the highway. There are two hundred acres of nature trails and picnic areas by the side of a lake that is home to geese. Logging relics are on the grounds.

REDWOOD DEMONSTRATION FORESTS

To show the diverse aims, methods, and benefits of industrial forest management within the redwood region, several firms have made demonstration forests available to the public. Tours are self-guided and there are restrooms and picnic areas available. You'll learn that only 1 percent of the tree is living—only the tips of its roots, the leaves, buds, flowers, seed, and a single thin layer of cells sheathing the tree. You see Douglas firs, white firs, and redwood residuals—the redwood trees that have sprung up from seeds and sprouts in three generations. Seven separate installations each tell the same story in a little different way:

Masonite Corporation's demonstration forest is just west of Navarro on Highway 128. One mile north of Rockport on Highway 1, the *Louisiana Pacific Corporation* provides a four-hundred-yard, twenty-minute walk along a scenic creek. Visit the *Pacific Lumber Company* four miles south of Scotia on Highway 101 and the *Simpson Timber Company,* one mile east of Blue Lake on Highway 299 to Redding. The *Samoa Division* of the Louisiana-Pacific Corporation is one mile north of Trinidad on *old* Highway 101.

Three miles south of Crescent City on Highway 101, the *Rellim Redwood Company* provides an excellent demonstration forest tour guide, showing logging history, reforestation, and identification drawings of the plants you'll see amid the redwoods.

CONFUSION HILL/MOUNTAIN TRAIN RIDE

Highway 101, Piercy. (707) 925-6456. Confusion Hill: daily 9–6; adults, $2; ages 6–12, $1; Mountain Train Ride: April–September. Adults, $2; ages 3–12, $1.

The miniature Mountain Train follows many switchbacks to take you one-and-one-quarter miles up to the summit of a redwood mountain, through a tunnel tree, and back down. Try the other experience at Confusion Hill—a spot where gravity is defied. You seem to be standing sideways; water runs uphill; your friends shrink or grow taller in front of you. Be sure to check out the Redwood Shoe. Nobody knows why all of this happens, but the kids are delighted by it.

PAT DERBY'S FAMOUS WILD ANIMALS (HOWLING WOLF LODGE)

Highway 101, Leggett. (707) 925-6211. By appointment only.

Pat Derby and Sweet William

Sweet William, black bear star of "Gentle Ben"; Stanley Goodwolf; Spot, a leopard that worked on "Daktari"; Christopher, the Mercury cougar; Ricochet, the Mercury bobcat; Harriet the Baboon; and other animals are put through their paces here by their glamorous trainer, Pat Derby. All of the animals are TV, movie, and commercial stars and you may even see some of them in action before the cameras during your visit. Rooms to rent and a small restaurant are also on the premises.

AVENUE OF THE GIANTS

Humboldt Redwoods State Park, Weott. (707) 946-2311. $2 day use; camping $6 per night.

Standing tall as a nominee for the most spectacular thirty-three miles anywhere is this bypass road winding leisurely beneath three-hundred-foot trees. One of the few tree species to have survived from the time of the dinosaurs, the redwoods are awesome, majestic trees to behold. You'll drive through a protected wilderness of soaring trees and moss and fern carpeted landscape occasionally spotted with deer. Founder's Grove, Rockefeller Forest, and Children's Forest are some of the best of the special groves. The Tree House in Piercy, Hobbiton and the Chimney Tree near Phillipsville, and the Drive-Thru Tree in Myers Flat are more commercial stopping places.

PACIFIC LUMBER COMPANY

Scotia, 27 miles south of Eureka. (707) 764-2222. Free museum and mill tours in summer, Monday–Thursday, 10–4.

Scotia is an old logging town that was built entirely of redwood. The museum, a fine old mansion, presents pictures of the loggers at work and play and a collection of logging equipment, tools, and relics. Here's where you get the pass for the self-guided tour of the mill, which takes about forty-five minutes and follows the processing of a log from the moment it comes off the truck. The first step is one of the most impressive—a debarker that uses water pressure to peel the log as if it were a banana. Many things go on all at once in the mill (which can be loud and more scary for timid adults than for the kids). The nearby Scotia Fish Rearing Pond, built by the lumber company to help rehabilitate the Eel River, raises 100,000 steelhead and salmon each year.

ALTON & PACIFIC RAILROAD

Highway 36, one-half mile east of Highway 101, Alton (Route 1, Box 477, Fortuna 95540.) No phone. Thursday–Tuesday, 11–5, Memorial Day through Labor Day. Adults, $2; ages 3–15, $1.25.

The Alton & Pacific Railroad is the only two-foot narrow gauge, wood-burning steam train on the West Coast and a ride on this rattling relic is a must for train buffs of any age. Minimum trip: at least four fares.

DEPOT MUSEUM

Park Street, Fortuna. (707) 725-2495. Daily 12–5 in summer; closed Thursday and Fridays, September–May. Donation.

The 1893 train depot is now a small museum housing Fortuna memories of the loggers, the farmers, the Indians, and the railroad. The old teletyper is at the ready; fancy dresses and shoes wait for the next dance; fishing poles and tackle stand waiting for the next fishing trip; and pictures and school books round out the collection. The three old marriage certificates are lovely. Visitors in the autumn may want to stop by Clendenen's Cider Works (Twelfth Street and Newberg Road, 725-2133) to see the mill in action and buy fresh cider. The Dollhouse Museum at 1710 Main Street (725-3738; 9–6 daily; adults 50¢, children 25¢) houses a remarkable collection of old and rare dollhouses and dollhouse furnishings including a mouse house with seashell beds, an 1880 German castle, a 1920 kitchen, and "The Old Lady Who Lived in a Shoe." Chapman's Gem and Mineral Shop and Museum, four miles south of the city on Highway 101 (725-4732), is open in summer, 10–5 daily.

FERNDALE MUSEUM

Shaw and 3rd Streets. Ferndale. (707) 786-4466. Tuesday–Saturday 12–4; Sunday, 1–4. Lectures and demonstrations by appointment.

A blacksmith shop with a working forge, antique farming and logging equipment, and a working seismograph are permanent exhibits, along with rotating collections that show the lifestyles, work habits, and activities of Ferndale's ancestors. Ferndale, a restored Victorian town, is a wonderful place to spend the day browsing.

CLARKE MEMORIAL MUSEUM

Third and E Streets, Eureka. (707) 443-1947. Tuesday–Saturday, 10–4. Free.

This large pioneer museum in a 1912 bank shows changing exhibits in airy, attractive new settings. Over 1,200 Indian baskets, gun collections, ships' bells, old typewriters, sewing machines, and antique dolls are displayed among mementos of early Humboldt County life, the maritime days, and from the Pomo Indians. The Clarke Memorial Museum is located in Eureka's *Old Town*, a restored section of town on the waterfront of Humboldt Bay. The commercial and residential Victorian buildings, crowned by the most photographed building in the west, the Carson Mansion (at Second and M) includes shops, boutiques, a gift shop in a railroad car, the Bon Bonniere Ice Cream Parlor at 215 F, Windjammer Books, and the Angelus at 420 Second, which specializes in music boxes and old dolls. If you want to see how oysters are processed, stop by at The Coast Oyster Company at the foot of A Street (9–2 Monday–Friday in winter, 442-2947) for a self-guided tour.

THE M/V MADAKET BAY TOUR

Sails from the foot of C Street, Eureka. 1, 2:30, and 4 P.M. in summer. (707) 442-3738. Adults, $3; ages 12–17, $2; 6–11, $1.50.

The seventy-five minute cruise aboard this venerable vessel takes in the oyster beds, pelican roosts, saw mills, egret rookery, former Indian village, and history of the area. An adults-only cocktail cruise sails at 5:30 on weekends.

SEQUOIA PARK AND ZOO

Glatt and W Streets, Eureka. (707) 443-7331. Tuesday–Sunday, 10–7 in summer, until 5 in winter. Closed on holidays. Free.

One hundred-fifty kinds of animals, mostly native to the area, are housed in this beautiful new zoo, the only one in the world in a redwood setting. There are river otters, Big Horn sheep, llamas, sitka deer, bear, birds, and chimpanzees; there's also a petting zoo for children. Playgrounds and picnic areas are available in the park.

FORT HUMBOLDT

3431 Fort Avenue, off Highway 101, Eureka. (707) 433-4588/443-7952. Daily 9–6. Free.

High on a windy hill overlooking a modern logging facility, Fort Humboldt is primarily an outdoor museum of the logging industry. Old machinery is accompanied by large billboards telling what it was like to be a logger in the nineteenth century. A logger's cabin is furnished with a stove, a bed, a shelf of beans, and a "pin-up" calendar. You learn how to "fall" a tree (the falling branches are called "widow makers"), then see how to drag it out of the forest and cut it up. One logger notes that it's "a shame to wash clothes while they can still bend." An 1884 Falk locomotive and an 1892 Andersonia locomotive are on view. Old Fort Humboldt, where U. S. Grant served as a staff officer in the 1850s, is nearby. A short film on the steam age of logging is shown regularly. A short drive away are the only two covered bridges in the area. Take 101 south to Elk River Road and follow along to either Zane or Bertas Road. The bridges are covered not to protect them from snow but to protect the lumber from rain—boarding them up preserves the wood longer and is less expensive than constant repainting.

SAMOA COOKHOUSE

Samoa Road, Eureka. (707) 442-1659. Breakfast: 7-11 A.M.; adults, $2.95; ages 7-11, $1.95; 3-6, $1.10. Lunch: 11-2 P.M.; adults, $2.85; ages 7-11, $1.85; 3-6,

$1.05. Dinner: 5-10 P.M.; adults, $5.75; ages 7-11, $3.25; 3-6, $1.95.

Family-style meals are served seven days a week in this old lumbercamp cookhouse which once served as relief quarters for shipwreck victims. The long tables are set as they were in 1900 with red-and-white checked cloths and large bottles of catsup. Our breakfast consisted of huge amounts of orange juice, coffee, delicious French toast, and made-by-hand sausages. Dinner the night before included thick cuts of ham and sole, and peach pie with all the fixings. Before or after the meal, wander through the adjoining rooms to see an assemblage of logger's boots, dinner bells, kitchen utensils, and a steam coffeemaker that once served five hundred men three times a day.

HUMBOLDT STATE UNIVERSITY MARINE LABORATORY

Trinidad. (707) 677-3671. Monday–Friday, 8–5; Saturday and Sunday 12–5 during the school year. Free.

Located at Land's End, in the picturesque fishing village of Trinidad, this working laboratory is open to the public for self-guided tours. Hallway aquariums hold rare and common molluscs and crustaceans, and fresh- and saltwater fish. Varicolored anemones, walleye surf perches, Siamese tigerfish, and shovel-nose catfish were there for our visit, along with a wolf eel that has been tamed and a small black octopus.

Do stop at the *Trinidad Lighthouse* on your way to the lab. This is the spot where the Spaniards landed on Trinity Sunday in 1775. The original gear system of descending weights still works to turn the light, but the original two-ton bell is for display only.

Patrick's Point State Park along the shore north of the laboratory boasts a small museum of Yurok artifacts and rock displays at park headquarters. (707) 677-3570. There is an admission for each car.

PRAIRIE CREEK REDWOODS STATE PARK

Highway 101, near Orick. (707) 488-2171.

Roosevelt elk roam this state park and can usually be seen grazing across the meadow from the Visitors Center. A small but interesting exhibit on the elk and the trees, ferns, flowers and animals of the area is on display. The most extraordinary object is a madrone tree that grew to envelope the skull of an elk.

Just south of the park, on 101, is the Prairie Creek Fish Hatchery (488-2253, 8–5 daily, free) which raises king and silver salmon and coastal cutthroat and rainbow trout.

Just north of Orick, at Bald Hills Road junction, the Arcata Redwood Company's Mill "A," welcomes visitors to view operations from overhead catwalks. A Forest Renewal Exhibit is five miles farther north.

TREES OF MYSTERY

Highway 101, Klamath. (707) 482-5613. 8 A.M. to 7 P.M. Monday–Friday; until 9 P.M. in summer; 8–5 daily in winter. Closed holidays. Adults, $4; ages 6-12, $2.

A talking forty-nine-foot Paul Bunyan greets you at the entrance, and then you walk through a hollowed redwood log into a forest of redwoods, where recorded music and explanations take you past trees such as "The Fallen Giant," and "The Elephant Tree," and the immense and moving "Cathedral Tree." Going back down the hill is our favorite section—Paul Bunyan's "Trail of Tall Tales," where you hear how Babe the Blue Ox was found, how the Grand Canyon was dug, and how Sourdough Sam makes his pancakes (his recipe includes the lard from one summer-fatted bear). The "End of the Trail" museum in the gift shop offers an array of baskets, clothes, and artifacts of tribes ranging from the Mississippi to the Pacific and north to the Aleutians.

The Tour-Thru Tree on Highway 101 at the north end of the Klamath River Bridge (known for its decorative golden bears) may be worth a short visit.

UNDERSEA WORLD

Highway 101 South, Crescent City. (707) 464-3522. Summer, 9–9 daily; winter, 9–5. Adults, $4.35; ages 12–15, $2.65. Group Rates available.

Over 5,000 marine specimens live in this habitat ten feet below sea level. The ferocious wolf eels, scurrying crabs, sun starfish, and black snappers that stand vertically to aid their digestion are all native to the area and presented in their normal environments. You'll see sables, big skates, starry flounders, and California sea lions, too. There's also a touchable tidepool exhibit and exhibits of dangerous sea creatures.

DEL NORTE HISTORICAL SOCIETY MUSEUM

577 H Street, Crescent City. (707) 464-3922. Monday–Saturday, 10–4 in summer and by appointment. Adults, $1.50.

The 1935 version of "Last of the Mohicans" was filmed in Crescent City and this museum, once the county jail, has many photos of the Indians who appeared in it. A Yurok bark house and stick games, headdresses, beads, dolls, and baskets of the Tolowa, Pomo, Hoopa, and Yurok tribes are shown, as are photos of Crescent City since its beginnings, with lots of "before and after" shots of the 1964 tidal wave. Unicycles, an early steam donkey used in logging, jail cells, local craftsmen's tools (including a moonshine still), pioneer clothing, and other collections by local residents will occupy your time here.

BATTERY POINT LIGHTHOUSE

Crescent City. Wednesday–Sunday, 10–4, at low tide. June–October. Free.

Battery Point Lighthouse is located offshore from Crescent City on a little island accessible only at low tide. The original light is still workable and the old log book, banjo clock, shipwreck photos, and nautical mementos add to the enjoyment of a visit. Although most children have hopes of being stranded by the tide, the wealth of native plants and view of the ocean from the tower will make up for their disappointment in finding themselves safely back on the Mainland.

SHIP ASHORE

Smith River. (707) 487-3141. 10–5:30 daily. Free.

This 160-foot former luxury yacht, which also served with the U.S. Navy during World War II, is now a landlocked gift shop with a complete naval and historical museum under the main deck. The wheel house is full of ship models—from a seventeenth century Man O'War to a World War II vessel— and kids can take a turn at the wheel itself. An autograph and the address of Nukuo Fujita, the only Japanese pilot to drop a firebomb on the United States, is on the wall. Downstairs you'll find a potpourri of memories and souvenirs that range from a 1910 country doctor's kit to Alaskan boots, stuffed owls and armadillos, an extensive shell collection, ship blueprints, swords and uniforms, clothes and necklaces from the Edward Lopez family of the Tolowa tribe, and a fascinating pirate's den that gives lore and rules pirates lived by.

PUBLIC RELATIONS TOURS

SIMPSON KORBEL FOREST NURSERY *Highway 299 near Blue Lake in Korbel. (707) 688-5621. Free tours daily, 11 A.M. and 1 P.M. in summer.*

MAD RIVER STATE FISH HATCHERY *Blue Lake. (707) 822-0592. By appointment.* Salmon and steelhead fish eggs, baby fish, and fingerlings may be seen by the drop-in visitor. By the way, the river is not ferocious. It was named for a fight between Joe Greeg and L. K. Wood, two explorers of the region, in 1849.

THE PENINSULA AND THE SAN JOSE AREA

The Peninsula and the San Jose area can provide many days of happy "attraction" hunting. There are huge amusement parks—such as Frontierland and Marriott's Great America—small museums, lovely parks, and interesting industries. A map showing city streets is helpful, and it might be a good idea to plan your day before you set out. Fast foods flourish on all the roads here, and picnic areas are always close by, so impromptu meals are easy.

SANCHEZ ADOBE

Linda Mar Boulevard, Pacifica. (415) 349-1462. Tuesday and Sunday 1–5 and by appointment. (574-6441). Free.

As the center of the Mission Dolores rancho and the site of the earliest Spanish settlement in San Mateo County, the Sanchez Adobe has lived through four periods of history which will soon be reflected in the buildings and restorations now in progress. Artifacts from the aboriginal Indians were discovered during an archaeological dig in 1978 and the San Mateo Historical Society hopes to put together an Indian village. The farmlands once produced the food for San Francisco's Mission Dolores and the mission outpost is now outlined on the adobe grounds. In 1842, Señor Sanchez, who served as the *alcalde,* or mayor, of San Francisco built his home here. The adobe still stands and is filled with his rancho mementos (especially in the tackroom/workroom downstairs) and the Victorian furniture and clothes of Sanchez's children and grandchildren.

COYOTE POINT MUSEUM FOR ENVIRONMENTAL EDUCATION

Coyote Point Park, San Mateo. (415) 342-7755. Wednesday–Friday, 10–5; weekends, 1–5. Adults, $1; seniors and ages 6–17, 50¢; children under 6 and everyone on Fridays, free. $2 car gate fee.

The Bay Area's only environmental science museum features a permanent exhibit with the world's largest bee tube plus aquarium, computer games, films, and a giant mural. The permanent exhibit introduces visitors to the beauty of the natural world, six major ecological concepts, and our relationship to the environment. The nearby Animal Center features animals native to the Bay Area (admission free).

JAPANESE TEA GARDEN

Central Park, San Mateo. (415) 377-4700. Monday–Friday, 9–4; weekends, 11–5. Free.

This proper, gracious Japanese garden is a soothing spot in the midst of city bustle. Quaint bridges and rock pathways take the visitor past a waterfall, a pond thick with waterlilies and goldfish, and, in the springtime, delicate cherry blossoms. The teahouse is open, irregularly, in summer.

San Mateo Japanese Tea Garden

SAN MATEO COUNTY HISTORICAL MUSEUM

1700 West Hillsdale Boulevard, College of San Mateo, San Mateo. (415) 574-6441. Wednesday–Friday, 9:30–4:30; Saturday and Sunday, 12:30–4:30. Free.

A walk through this museum is a walk through history. You begin with the Pleistocene period—14 million years ago—and view bones and fossils found in San Mateo from that age. Then on to the Costanoan Indians of 3,000 years ago, and the description of their magic dances, boats, tools, and food. The Mission Rancho period is well-represented and exhibits of lumber mills, an old general store and bar, settlers' wagons, and unicycles speak for the pioneers. An 1860s kitchen and 1880 Victorian living room are being designed.

FARRELL'S ICE CREAM PARLOUR

109 Bovet Road, San Mateo. (415) 345-1894. Sunday–Thursday, 11–11; Friday and Saturday until 12.

Farrell's brings all of a child's fantasies to life in its birthday extravaganzas. Drums pound, whistles and bells blow, candles are lit, and the entire restaurant sings to the birthday child. The birthday party Zoo sundae of eight ice creams, five sherbets, five toppings, almonds, whipped cream, cherries, and bananas goes for $18.50 and comes with at least ten spoons. Other Farrell's favorites start at $1.75 for an old-fashioned soda, shake, or sundae (soda water is still 2¢ plain) and end with the Pig's Trough. There's a special award if you finish this one by yourself. Sandwiches of all kinds are available, too.

There are other Farrell's in Sunnyvale, Fremont, Sacramento, Hayward, Fresno, and Daly City's Serramonte Shopping Center.

MARINE WORLD/AFRICA USA

Marine World Parkway off Bayshore Freeway, Redwood City. (415) 365-7446/ DOLPHIN. Daily 9:30-6 in summer, closed Monday and Tuesday during spring and fall; open weekends only in winter. Adults $7.50; ages 5-12 $4.50; covers all shows.

Marine World/Africa USA is a day-long adventure. Although the price may seem high, you'll find that the family can spend the entire day there happily and not pay for anything else except food, which you can pack along. Shows are scheduled so you can go from one to another at an easy pace. You can watch trained whales and jungle cats, cheer the Dolphin Olympics, take a river raft, pet a porpoise or an aoudad, wander through a fun-filled bird jungle, and see water-ski shows and puppet shows.

MARINE ECOLOGICAL INSTITUTE

285 Seaport Boulevard, Redwood City. (415) 364-2760.

Tours aboard the eighty-five-foot research vessel *Inland Seas* offer an introduction to the delicate ecology of San Francisco Bay and the Delta. Instructors point out marsh and marine life, discuss currents and waves, pollution, land fill, and planning. Half-day discovery voyage.

FILOLI HOUSE AND GARDEN TOURS

Canada Road, Woodside. (415) 366-2880. Two-hour docent-led tours, 3 times a day, by reservation. $6. Children under 12 not allowed.

Walk through the house and garden that star in TV's "Dynasty"—43 rooms of Georgian-style mansion and 17 acres of formal gardens.

Filoli Nature Hikes (366-4640; Monday, Thursday, and Saturday at 9:30, by reservation; adults, $3; children, with adult only, $1). In Filoli's back country you can learn about the Indians who lived there; touch the San Andreas faultline; and learn about the animals, plants, and history of the area. The two-hour hikes are two or three miles long.

WEST BAY MODEL RAILROAD CLUB

1090 Merrill Street, Menlo Park. (415) 322-0685.

Three different-sized trains run on the club's four thousand feet of track, whistling past miniature towns and painted scenery and over tiny bridges and turntables. Adding to the effectiveness of the show is a tape of special sound effects interspersed with the story of how the club came about. The club also has a railroad-stationery display, a library, and a machine shop. The members' special Christmas show on a December weekend is a favorite event for local youngsters.

STANFORD UNIVERSITY

Stanford Campus, Palo Alto. (415) 497-2300. Stanford Guide Service in the Hoover Institute Lobby, 497-2053: Monday–Saturday, 9–5; Sunday, 10–4. Stanford Linear Accelerator Center by appointment, 854-3300, ext. 2204. Hoover Institution on War, Revolution and Peace, 497-2053: Monday–Saturday, 9–5, free. Observatory platform, 50¢; Monday–Saturday, 10–12 and 1–4; Sunday, 1–4. Seniors get 25 percent discount, children under 12 free. Leland Stanford, Jr., Museum, 497-4177: Tuesday–Friday, 10–4:45; weekends, 1–4:45, free.

In addition to the lovely view from the tower, the Hoover Institute offers memories of Herbert Hoover and his White House years and world crusades. A settee and chairs that belonged to Abraham Lincoln are also on view. Remembrances of the Stanford family are displayed in the luxurious building, *Leland Stanford, Jr., Museum (497-4177,Tuesday–Friday, 10–4:45; weekends 1-4:45; free)*, along with a widely varied collection of Indian artifacts; European and primitive art and sculpture; a jade collection; and an Egyptorium, with a mummy in an open case. The Stanford Rooms feature toy trains and soldiers, a check signed by George Washington, children's books, weapons, archaeological findings from Pompeii, and Mrs. Stanford's gowns. The original "Gold Spike," driven in 1869 to complete the nation's first transcontinental railroad, is in a special case.

BAYLANDS NATURE INTERPRETIVE CENTER

At the eastern end of Embarcadero Road, Palo Alto. (415) 329-2506. Wednesday–Friday, 2–5; weekends, 1–5. Free. (Mailing address: c/o Palo Alto Junior Museum.)
This bayside nature center is on the pilings out in a salt marsh, handy

for the nature walks and ecology workshops it excels in. The exhibits show local birds, plants, and a saltwater aquarium. On weekends, there are nature movies and slide lectures, as well as conducted nature and bird walks, bike tours, wildflower shows, fish, pond, and geology programs.

PALO ALTO JUNIOR MUSEUM AND ZOO

Rinconada Park, 1451 Middlefield Road, Palo Alto. (415) 329-2111. Tuesday–Friday, 10–12, 1–5; Saturday, 10–5; Sunday 1–4. Free.

This beautifully constructed museum has constantly changing exhibits to keep kids coming back for more. Outside, in the poured concrete shelters, there are snakes and reptiles, ravens, owls and foxes, and lovable rabbits. Ducks nest under the bridge that curves over the pretty pond. The exhibitions program focuses on physical, biological, and earth science.

Feeding time at the Children's Zoo

FOOTHILL COLLEGE ELECTRONICS MUSEUM

12345 El Monte Road, Foothill College, Los Altos Hills. (415) 948-8590, ext. 383.

Thursday and Friday, 9–12 and 1–4:30; Sunday, 1–4:30. Adults, $2; children, 50¢.

The most complete collection of ancient radio tubes, spark transmitters, and klytrons in the world is now open to radio hobbyists of all ages. Special exhibits that allow visitors to experiment with tubes, transmitters, and receivers are most popular. Computers, video recorders, calculators, and the very first commercial radio broadcasting station the world ever listened to are on display as well.

ENGINE HOUSE

672 Alberta, near Hollenbach and Fremont, Sunnyvale. (408) 245-0609. Wednesday–Friday, 12–5; Saturday, 10–5; Sunday, 12–5; longer hours in summer and just before Christmas.

One million items ("the next million we have on order") of interest to train fans are crammed into this treasure-filled space. Cars, kits, photos, hobby magazines, models of trains from old wood-burners to BART, and everything you'd need to create a complete train world can be found in this, the largest train shop in the west. Nearby, the Sunnyvale Historical Museum (235 East California Avenue, 739-3642) is open daily, except Wednesday and is free.

MINOLTA PLANETARIUM

De Anza College, 21250 Stevens Creek Boulevard and Stelling Road, Cupertino. (408) 996-4814. Special changing shows on Tuesday and Thursday through Sunday, with different prices.

The Minolta Planetarium employs the latest audiovisual equipment and techniques to present remarkable shows. The main projector spreads the night sky across a fifty-foot dome, and twenty-four sound speakers and 150 other projectors are used to produce some dazzling effects. These mechanical marvels take you not only through space but through time; you fly to the moon to look at the brilliance of the stars as they were seen by the astronauts, then you travel back in time to see how the stars looked to man when he first saw them. It's a wondrous experience that combines education and entertainment.

The new Environmental Studies Area, open 12–4 on the first Saturday of each month and by appointment, provides a variety of biological environments representing major communities in California.

Le Petit Trianon Museum (996-4712) features rotating exhibits on California history.

HAKONE JAPANESE GARDENS

21000 Big Basin Way, Saratoga. (408) 867-3438, ext. 50. Monday–Friday, 10–5; Saturday and Sunday, 11–5; closed holidays. Teahouse open in summer, 25¢.

Walk along curving foliage-lined paths, through a wisteria-covered arbor, step on three stones to get across a stream next to three waterfalls.

Climb a moon bridge to see the goldfish. Discover little houses and gazebos hidden in the trees. Spy stone and wooden lanterns, statues of cranes, and cats hidden in the foliage. Rest in a peaceful, tatami-matted teahouse overlooking shaped trees. Sit in a wisteria-roofed summerhouse. This wonderful garden was designed by a former court gardener to the Emperor of Japan as a hill and water garden, the strolling pond style typical of Zen gardens in the seventeenth century.

The Saratoga Historical Park and Museum (20450 South Saratoga–Los Gatos Road, Saratoga, 867-4311) is worth a stop.

VILLA MONTALVO

Saratoga–Los Gatos Road, Saratoga. (408) 867-3421. Arboretum, Monday–Friday, 8–5; Saturday and Sunday, 9–5. Galleries: Thursday–Saturday, 1–4; Sunday 11–4. Summer, Wednesday, 11–3.

Nature trails traverse a redwood grove, hills and meadows, and flower-covered arbors in this county-run, privately-held arboretum. The villa's grounds are also a bird sanctuary for up to forty-one species of birds. The villa takes its name from a sixteenth-century Spanish author. Montalvo wrote a novel describing a tribe of Amazons living in a fabulous island paradise named "California"! The Amazons rode on gryphons, and the many stone gryphons on the grounds are sure to entrance youngsters. Storytelling, music, dance, and other performing arts events are scheduled in spring and summer.

PAUL MASSON VINEYARDS

13150 Saratoga Avenue, Saratoga. (408) 725 4270. Daily 10–4. Free.

Display cabinets of rare wine vessels and glasses—some dating back to 1000 B.C.—and the slide show of the history of Paul Masson and his wine add information and pleasure to the self-guided tour offered here. In summers, there are jazz and classical music concerts at the nearby mountain winery.

BILLY JONES WILDCAT RAILROAD

Oak Meadow Park, Los Gatos. (408) 349-9775. Daily except Monday, 11–5:30 in summer, and spring and fall weekends. 50¢.

A full steam narrow-gauge, eighteen-inch prairie-type railroad toots along a mile-long track pulling four open cars. The short ride takes you into the forest, near a stream, and back to the busy city park.

LOS GATOS MUSEUM

Tait and Main Streets, Los Gatos. (408) 354-2646. Winter: Monday–Friday, 1–4; Saturday and Sunday, 10–4; Summer, 10–4 daily. Tours by appointment. Free.

The art section of this welcoming museum features constantly changing historical and contemporary art exhibits. The natural history room has a fluorescent minerals exhibit and a table where you can touch petrified wood, talc, Indian mortars, and a fossil whale vertebra. The star of the show is the beehive. A glass cage surrounds this thriving hive on all sides except for the outer wall. You can stand for hours watching the bees fly in and out, filling and eating their honeycomb. If you're very quiet, you can even hear them singing.

MISSION SANTA CLARA DE ASIS

University of Santa Clara, the Alameda, 820 Alviso, Santa Clara. (408) 984-4242. Daily, 7 A.M.–7 P.M. Free.

Founded in 1777 and now part of the university campus, the present mission is a replica of the third building raised on this site by the mission fathers. An adobe wall from the original cloister still stands in the peaceful garden. The original cross of the mission stands in front of the church, and the bell given by the King of Spain in 1778 still tolls.

The de Saisset Gallery (Tuesday–Friday, 10–5; weekends, 1–5) and Ricard Observatory (10–2 Wednesday) are on the campus and make interesting short stops.

ROSICRUCIAN EGYPTIAN MUSEUM, SCIENCE MUSEUM, AND PLANETARIUM

Rosicrucian Park, Naglee and Park Avenues, San Jose. (408) 287-9171. Egyptian Museum: Tuesday–Friday, 9–4:45; Saturday—Monday, 12–4:45. Adults, $2.50; ages 12–17, $1. Science Museum: Wednesday–Sunday, 1–5 in summer; weekends only in winter. Free. Planetarium shows: Monday–Saturday, 2 and 3:30; Sunday, 1, 2:30, and 4. Planetarium itself is open on summer weekends, 12–5. Adults, $2; ages 12–17, $1; under 12 and school groups free.

The wonderful, faraway world of ancient Egypt awaits to mystify and enchant you in a collection at least ten times larger than the King Tut show. Egyptian and Babylonian mummies, sculpture, paintings, jewelry, cosmetics, scarabs, scrolls, and amulets are here in abundance. The ornate coffins, mummified cats and falcons, and descriptions of the embalming process are totally absorbing. Our four-year-old kept wanting to know how "old" everybody was. A short tour takes you inside a rock tomb, the only one on the West Coast, through the outer hallways and into the crypt to see wall paintings, false doorways, and the sarcophagus itself. Dioramas and lifelike models show the manner in which the ancient Egyptians lived.

There's a seismograph and a Foucault pendulum in the science museum next door, along with lifelike models of satellites, neighboring planets, moons, and the solar system, with lots of buttons to push on exhibits demonstrating the fundamental laws of the physical sciences. Planetarium shows change regularly.

WINCHESTER MYSTERY HOUSE

525 South Winchester Boulevard, San Jose. (408) 247-2101. Tours daily, 9–4:30 in winter, till 6 in summer. House and grounds: adults, $7.95; ages 6–12, $4.95; seniors, $6.45. House tour: adults, $3.50; children, $2. Both tours include the museum. Museum only: adults, $1; children, 75¢.

Sarah Winchester, widow of the Winchester Rifle heir, was told that as long as she kept building something, she'd never die. So for thirty-eight years, carpenters worked twenty-four hours a day to build this 160-room mansion filled with mysteries. Doorways open to blank walls, secret passageways twist around, and the number thirteen appears everywhere—thirteen-stepped stairways, ceilings with thirteen panels, rooms with thirteen windows—all in the finest woods and crystals money could buy. The museum features lifesize wax dioramas of the Winchesters and some of the people who used their hardware: Annie Oakley and Buffalo Bill, Butch Cassidy and the Sundance Kid, and Teddy Roosevelt.

SAN JOSE HISTORICAL MUSEUM

635 Phelan Avenue, Kelley Park, San Jose. (408) 287 2290. Tuesday–Friday, 10–4:30; weekends, 12–4:30. Adults, $1; children and seniors, 50¢. Tours by appointment.

Historic San Jose offers a unique view of the past, a visit to the heart of San Jose much as it existed in the nineteenth century. On sixteen acres surrounding a quiet plaza, original and faithfully replicated homes and businesses present the past in a lively manner. O'Brien's Candy Store still serves candy and sodas; the print shop looks as if it could put out a paper tomorrow; the blacksmith works away in Dashaway Stables; and you can walk through or past the Bank of Italy, the Umbarger House, the 115-foot Electric Light Tower, the Firehouse, and the Doctor's office. The Pacific Hotel houses a "proper" museum tracing the people of the Santa Clara Valley, from the Ohlone Indians to the Spanish and Mexican *vaqueros* and *rancheros*, and the Yankee pioneers. Chinatown San Jose, an 1885 nickelodeon, and a nickel movie of the San Francisco earthquake are shown, along with a slanted narrow ladder once used in the New Almaden quicksilver mine.

True history buffs will want to drive over to see the Roberto Adobe, built in 1836, at 770 Lincoln Avenue, and the Peralta Adobe, at 184 West St. John Street, built in 1775, the sole structure remaining from the Spanish period.

JAPANESE FRIENDSHIP TEA GARDEN

1490 Senter Road, Kelley Park, San Jose. (408) 286-3626. Daily, 10–6, later in summer. Free.

This tranquil garden is patterned after the Korakuen garden in San Jose's sister city of Okayama. The three lakes are designed to symbolize the word "kokoro," which means "heart-mind-and-soul." Picturesque bridges and waterfalls, shaped rocks and trees, and land and waterflowers are wonderful to wander around. Naturally, the children will head over to watch the families of *koi*, magnificent, fat gold, white or black carp who come when dinner is offered.

From the Tea Garden or the Historical Museum, you can take the Southern Pacific Coast Rail Road Train through Kelley Park to the next stop. Trains leave every half hour on the hour and the rides are 50¢.

HAPPY HOLLOW PARK AND BABY ZOO

Kelley Park, Keyes and Senter Roads, San Jose. (408) 292-8188/295-8383. Daily, 10–4; Sunday, 11–6. Adults, $1.25; children, 75¢.

A miniature Viking shop, gingerbread house, and King Arthur's castle are some of the attractions in this delightful children's park. There are places to climb, crooked miles to walk, animals to pet, a happy-go-round or Danny the Dragon to ride, and puppet shows to laugh at. The Zoo is inhabited by dwarf zebras, lemurs, Scottish Highland cows, Barbados sheep, pigmy horses, and goats, which are all there to be petted. Birds, monkeys, and seals are viewable in the beautifully landscaped zoo itself. Picnic areas are available in Kelley Park.

WORLD OF MINIATURES

1373 South Bascom, San Jose. (408) 294-2166. Adults, $3.95; children, $1.95; seniors, $3.25. Tuesday–Saturday, 10:30–5:30; Sunday, 12–5.

A Victorian city with houses, hotels, stores, and an amusement park with working train and carousel and a Hall of Rooms ranging from Paul Revere's drawing room to a modern fantasy bedroom—all done on a one-inch scale— will fascinate the whole family. Kids will especially enjoy playing with the five model trains.

YOUTH SCIENTIFIC INSTITUTE

Alum Rock Park, San Jose. (408) 258-4322. Tuesday–Friday, 9–4:30; Saturday, 12–4:30. On summer Sundays, 11–5:30. Adults, 50¢; children, 10¢; families, $1.

A small petting area and a hands-on exhibit of whale bones and shark teeth will draw the children, as will the hawks, owls, ravens, kestrels, snakes, newts, skunks, boa constrictors, chinchillas, and chipmunks.

NEW ALMADEN MUSEUM

21570 Almaden Road, New Almaden. (408) 268-7869. Monday, Thursday, and Friday, 1–4; Saturday, Sunday, and holidays, 10–5 and by appointment. Adults, $3; seniors, $2.50; ages 11–12, $1; 6–10, 75¢.

The New Almaden mine was the first mercury mine in California. The woman who owns the mine has gathered together mementos of the Indians, Mexicans, and American pioneers who lived in the area. She gives tour-talks through the museum, telling stories about the Indian dresses and artifacts, miners' tools and lunch pails, antique toys, sample ores, and old Mexican keepsakes. The barrel organ used by the padres to attract the Indians is of special interest.

Happy Hollow—San Jose

FLYING LADY No. II AND WAGONS TO WINGS COLLECTION

Hill Country Showplace Golf Course, 15060 Foothill Road, Morgan Hill. (408) 779-4136.

The Flying Lady restaurant is remarkable for its relaxing golf course setting and the model plane and picture collection covering its walls and ceiling. Two large buildings on the property house phenomenal collections of planes and wagons. We found a 1920 Briggs and Stratton Flier that got 100 miles per gallon, a 1928 Gypsy Moth, a Hupmobile, biplanes, war planes, jet planes, and a one-man folding helicopter. Buckboards, a graceful white hearse, a popcorn vender, stagecoaches, surreys, a dairy cart, and more in the "horse-drawn" barn.

Further down 101, in Gilroy, you may want to stop in at the Gilroy Historical Museum (195 Fifth Street, (408) 847-2685; 10–4 except Tuesday and Sunday; donation) to see its collection of local remembrances and Native American artifacts.

LICK OBSERVATORY

Mount Hamilton, Highway 130, 25 miles southeast of San Jose. (408) 274-5061 (recording); 429-2513. Visitors gallery 10–5 daily; tours, 1–5; closed holidays. Free.

A long narrow, winding road takes you to the top of Mount Hamilton and the awesome domes of Lick Observatory. It was here that the fifth moon of Jupiter was discovered—the first new one since the time of Galileo. The visitor's gallery looks up at one of the largest telescopes (120 inches) in the world, and the tour of photos and the telescopes, astronomical instruments, and 36-inch refractor is intriguing and educational. Star gazing is possible for the public on Friday nights in summer, but you must write (enclosing a self-addressed, stamped envelope, for up to six tickets) in advance to Visitors Program, Lick Observatory, Mt. Hamilton, CA 95140.

World of Miniatures

PUBLIC RELATIONS TOURS

ACRES OF ORCHIDS. *Rod McLellan Orchidary. 1450 El Camino Real, South San Francisco. (415) 871-5655. Guided tours 10:30 and 1:30 daily.* Orchids in more colors, types, and sizes than you can imagine are here in varying stages for looking, smelling, and buying.

EDELWEISS DAIRY. *17717 Old Mountain View Road, Santa Clara. (408) 984-8484. Monday–Saturday, 9–5 by appointment. Free.* Here you'll see the milking process from cow to carton.

U.S. WEATHER SERVICE. *Bayshore Freeway, San Bruno. San Francisco International Airport. (415) 876-2886. Free tours, by appointment.* See the materials used in briefing pilots and the weather teletypes and instruments. To see San Francisco Airport itself, call 761-0800 for a ninety-minute tour.

PALO ALTO AIRPORT. *1925 Embarcadero Road, Palo Alto. (415) 856-7833. By appointment. Free.* You can even get into the control tower if you make an additional call and appointment at 856-1277.

FRITO-LAY POTATO CHIPS. *650 North King Road, San Jose. (408) 251-8080. Write for reservations. Free.* Thirty-minute tours show how potato chips are made.

SUNSET MAGAZINE. *Middlefield and Willow Roads, Menlo Park. (415) 321-3600. Tours Monday–Friday, 10:30, 11:30, 1, 2. and 3. Gardens open 9–4:30. Free.* Cliff May designed the Sunset buildings to give the staff a good view and prevent glare. The garden itself is what the children like best: They can walk from one end to the other and view, in order, the botanical life of the western coast of America—the desert plants of Baja, the cactus of Southern California, the coastal shrubs of Monterey, and the rhododendrons and sturdy trees of Oregon and Washington. Youngsters with an interest in journalism will learn that working on a magazine is not all glamour.

NASA AMES RESEARCH CENTER. *Moffett Field, Mountain View. (415) 965-6497. By appointment. Free.* For ages 9 and up, a thirty-minute film and walking tour of the world's largest wind tunnel, space vehicles, and other research facilities can be fascinating. At certain times, you can also see the centrifuge flight simulation facilities and research aircraft.

THE SANTA CRUZ AREA

The Santa Cruz Area is small, nestled west of San Jose and north of Monterey. Big Basin Redwoods, Boulder Creek, and Loch Lomond are some of the natural sites of interest, and the villages of Watsonville and Castroville, home of the artichoke, are warm and welcoming. In Santa Cruz, beaches are the major interest. Be sure to have some car games with you—the drive from San Francisco can be long and slow.

SANTA CRUZ BEACH AND BOARDWALK

Riverside Avenue and Beach Street, Santa Cruz. (408) 426-7433. Daily, 11–11 in summer; weekends, 11–11 on Saturday; 11–7 on Sunday. Closed Christmas weekend.

Our eleven-year-old nephew calls the Giant Dipper roller coaster "a must." That's what I say about the 1911 merry-go-round with the authentic pipe organ and real brass rings. Last of the old-time boardwalks, Santa Cruz has everything you would hope to find on one: a Ferris wheel, bumper cars, skeet ball, miniature golf, a penny arcade, cotton candy, candied apples, corndogs, tacos, and gentle and stomach-churning rides. Crowds and prices change with the seasons.

The sand on the beach is white and welcoming and leads to the Santa Cruz Wharf, a great spot to fish and watch seals snoozing on the wharf pilings.

The pretty little Mark Abbott Memorial lighthouse on Lighthouse Point marks the boundary of the Pacific Ocean and Monterey Bay and shelters a tiny museum that is open weekend afternoons.

THE MYSTERY SPOT

1953 Banciforte Drive, Santa Cruz. (408) 423-8897. Daily, 9:30–4:30. Adults, $2.50; under 12, $1.25. Group rates.

All the laws of gravity seem to be challenged in this scary natural curiosity. Even the trees can't stand up straight, and a visitor always seems to be standing either backwards or sideways. One test here is to lay a carpenter's level across two cement blocks, checking to see that their tops are on the same level. Then stand on one and see your friend on the other suddenly shrink or grow tall. Our kids got a great kick out of walking up the walls of the cabin that looks cockeyed, but isn't.

SANTA CRUZ CITY MUSEUM

1305 East Cliff Drive, Santa Cruz. (408) 429-3773. Tuesday–Saturday, 10–5. Tourists, $1; residents, 50¢; children and seniors, free.

See natural history exhibits of animals, birds, and plant groups by natural community in beautiful displays. Learn how local Ohlone Indians lived; you can grind acorns in a stone mortar. See an ancient mammoth tusk and a mastodon skull from prehistoric denizens of the region. Touch live tidepool animals. Climb on the life-sized gray whale on the lawn and picnic in the park that surrounds the museum. Build a sand castle on the beach across the street.

In town, the Cooper House in the Pacific Garden Mall is the old county courthouse transformed into a bazaar of shops that's a feast for the eye and the palate: cafes, a rainbow store, pet shop, and strolling musicians make it a good place to while away a rainy afternoon.

You might also enjoy a stop at the Santa Cruz Arts Center, on Center Street, or the tiny Historical Museum of Santa Cruz (Cooper and Front Street; (408) 425-2540; Tuesday–Saturday, 12–5) in the octagon-shaped old county hall.

ROARING CAMP AND BIG TREES NARROW GAUGE RAILROAD

Graham Hill and Mount Hermon Roads, Felton. (408) 335-4484. Winter: weekdays at noon; weekends and holidays at 12, 1:30, and 3. Spring and fall: weekdays at noon; weekends and holidays (and daily throughout the summer) at 11, 12:15, 1:30, 2:45, and 4 P.M. Closed Christmas Day. Moonlight parties, summer Saturdays and by appointment. Adults, $7.95; ages 3–15, $5.50.

Curving through redwood forests and over rattling wooden trestles, the original 1880 steam engine pulls old-fashioned excursion cars up and down hills and around sky-high trees. You can stop over at Bear Mountain to hike and picnic before returning to Roaring Camp on a later train. Back at the Camp, the shortest covered bridge in the world and a duck pond interest younger folk, while the Old General Store—offering pot-bellied stoves, cast-iron toys, stick candy, and railroad books and magazines—intrigues the rest. Picnic tables and group rates are available.

PAJARO VALLEY HISTORICAL ASSOCIATION

226 East Beach Street, Watsonville. (408) 722-0305. Tuesday, Wednesday, and Thursday, 11–3; Saturday, 1–4; and by appointment. Free.

This is truly a community museum. One of the biggest treasures is a large 1887 photograph of two young girls—who are now members of the historical society. Reticules, bisque dolls, glove boxes used by the ladies of the town, and a photo of the first telephone office in Watsonville are part of the changing displays. Two old candy jars still filled with forty-year-old candy always capture the children's attention.

Roaring Camp and Big Trees Railroad

THE MONTEREY AREA

The Monterey area is many things—it's an Arcadian seashore; a farm-rich industrial city; and a sweeping, windswept valley. Monterey is also the site of the first important Spanish settlement in California, and it was here that the state of California became part of the United States. Big Sur has probably the most magnificent seacoast in the United States. Salinas, the city most of us know from Steinbeck's *East of Eden,* has fascinating industrial tours and many memories of Steinbeck himself. And the valley that sweeps south to Soledad Mission, past Pinnacles National Monument and on past San Antonio de Padua Mission, is just now being developed as fertile farm land. A day, or a weekend, in this area could never do it justice.

SAN JUAN BAUTISTA STATE HISTORIC PARK

San Juan Bautista. (408) 623-4881. Daily, 10–4:30 in winter, until 5 in summer. Tickets, usable in all state parks that day: Adults, 50¢; children, 25¢.

A mission, a museum, an adobe house, an 1870s hotel and stables, a wash house, blacksmith shop, granary, and wine-tasting room all encircle the lovely plaza of San Juan Bautista, representing three periods in California history—Spanish, Mexican, and early Californian.

Start your visit at the *Mission,* founded in 1797 and carefully preserved. The old adobe rooms house many treasures, including a 1737 barrel organ, gaming sticks of the San Juan Indians, the original kitchen, and rawhide thongs and hand-shaped nails from the original building. The original bells still call parishioners to daily mass. The rose gardens and olive groves are peaceful retreats, as is the Indian burial ground behind the church. The church itself is bright and colorful, painted by a sailor who jumped ship and became the first American citizen to settle in California.

Across the plaza is the *Zanetta House,* which once housed the Indian maidens of the settlement. The second floor was used as a public meeting room and dance hall. Visitors see fine china on the dining room table, a unique rocker in the living room, and furnished bedrooms. Pass the wash house and adobe cottage to the *Livery Stables,* where you can have fun rummaging through an assortment of carriages, wagons, harnesses, and mail pouches. The stables also house General Castro's secretary's office. *The Plaza Hotel,* next, is noted for its barroom, with billiard and poker tables standing ready. Built in 1813 as a barracks for the Spanish soldiers, the walls now display Wells Fargo memorabilia and photos and drawings of Indians, outlaws, and Mexican and Yankee pioneers.

The *Castro House* should serve as a model for other museums: Every room is completely labeled, with pictures to aid in the identification of its objects. The house is furnished as it was in the 1870s by the Breen family, who survived the Donner Party disaster to find a fortune in the gold fields. You'll see the candlesticks that came West with the Breens and the diary, wardrobe, wedding dress, gloves, fan, orange blossoms, and card case of Isabella Breen. The kitchen is complete, down to the mouse trap on the floor and the laundry board in the sink.

The streets near the Plaza are full of old adobes and small interesting shops and restaurants, making San Juan Bautista a perfect place to spend a relaxing day.

SAN LUIS RESERVOIR

Romero Overlook, Highway 152, between Hollister and Los Banos. (209) 826-1196. Open sunrise to 10 P.M.; closed holidays.

The history of this $600-million project is spread out before you, from Indian artifacts found during the digging of the dam to the plant and viewing window of the generator. Movies and slide shows on water conservation and the water project are shown, and a ranger will answer questions.

MONTEREY

Monterey's recorded history started when Cabrillo sighted the Bay of Piños in 1542. Today it's a bustling town ringing with history and always looking at the bay.

Fisherman's Wharf is a melange of restaurants, fish stores, and shops. Fishing and seal watching are favorite pastimes and you can go for a boat ride or take a diving bell thirty feet down to look at the ocean's floor.

Cannery Row is a far cry from the Cannery Row John Steinbeck told us about. This is a growing complex of restaurants, shops and galleries offering entertainment for all. It's here you'll find "The Funnest Place in Town!"— the Edgewater Packing Company and its 1905 Colossal Carrousel (640 Wave Street; (408) 649-1899; 8 A.M.–11 P.M., longer hours on summer weekends). You can ride a unicorn, listen to the loud calliope, and look at the sea on the carrousel's surprisingly fast, long ride. On the other side of the arcade is a restaurant and an ice cream and pie shop with fifteen kinds of pie and cake and deliciously old-fashioned ice cream concoctions. The flaming banana split is $2.95 and is served in a ceramic banana. Kids' parties are held in the old fire engine.

The Wax Museum (700 Cannery Row, 11 A.M.–11 P.M.) features vignettes of Cannery Row from 1550 to Steinbeck's day.

MONTEREY BAY AQUARIUM

886 Cannery Row, Monterey. (408) 649-6466. 10 A.M. to 6 P.M. daily except Christmas. Adults, $7; students and seniors, $5; children 3–12, $3.

In this startling undersea tour of Monterey Bay, visitors will meet 300 living species in 23 habitat galleries and exhibits, including a three-story high kelp forest. California sea otters frolic nose to nose with you in one section. You can investigate with telescopes and microscopes, play with bat rays, or walk through a shorebird aviary. Since the Monterey Aquarium is one of the leading attractions on the coast it's a good idea to buy tickets ahead of time through Ticketron.

SANCHO PANZA RESTAURANT

Casa Gutierrez, 590 Calle Principal, Monterey. (408) 375-0095. Daily 11–2 and 5–9. Open later on summer weekends.

Casa Gutierrez is a unit of the Monterey State Historic Park. By following the "Path of History," visitors can find their way to any of 42 historic adobe buildings. The head office of Monterey State Historic Park is at 210 Oliver Street. One state park ticket may be used in all the buildings throughout the day.

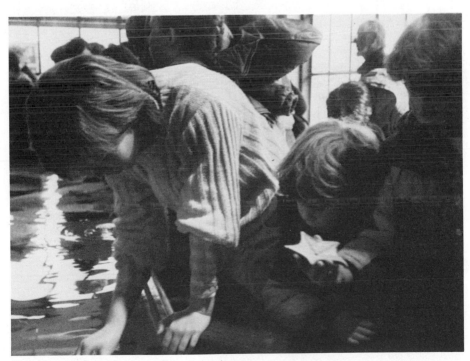

Teaching pool at Monterey Bay Aquarium

Built in 1841 by a young Mexican for his bride, the old adobe is now a comfortable Mexican country inn that looks like an early Monterey home. A warm fire blazes on cool evenings and there's a garden in back for lunch and summer nights. Prices are reasonable and the food is good. Mexican-American newspapers are used as placemats and conversation pieces. At the end of the meal, top it off with Chocolate Mejicano—crushed almonds and cinnamon in frothy hot chocolate.

ALLEN KNIGHT MARITIME MUSEUM

550 Calle Principal, Monterey. (408) 375-2553. Tuesday–Friday, 1–4; weekends, 2–4. Free.

A captain's cabin from an old sailing ship with bed, writing desk, and sailor's ditty box sets the proper mood for this nautical museum. Models, photos, lithographs, paintings and various old sailing materials, octants, ships' bells, sailors' thimbles, Arctic goggles, scrimshaw, and ships' logs are some of the items on display. One exhibit pictures all the ships that have visited Monterey harbor. There's even a sardine boat in which you can pretend you're sailing.

THE LARKIN HOUSE

Jefferson Street and Calle Principal, Monterey. (408) 649-2836. Thirty-five-minute guided tours from 10 to 4. Garden open until 5. Adult state parks ticket, $1.

Built by Thomas Oliver Larkin, first and only U.S. Consul to Mexico stationed in Monterey, the house is an architectural and historical gem. It was the first home in Monterey to follow the New England style as well as the first to have glass windows. Many of the furnishings are original Larkin items.

Through the rose-covered garden is a small house used by William Tecumseh Sherman, an army lieutenant in 1847–1849. The house now serves as a waiting room for the Larkin House tour and as a small museum of Sherman's and Larkin's roles in California history. Here you learn that Sherman promised to return to lovely Doña Maria Ignacio Bonifacio. She planted a rose to bloom when he returned. And although the Sherman rose has bloomed yearly ever since, the man who marched through Georgia never returned.

On the next block, the *Cooper-Molera House* (at the corner of Polk and Munras) will soon be open to the public. John B. R. Cooper, trader and sea captain, came to Monterey in the 1920s; married the daughter of Ignacio Vallejo; and founded a dynasty of farm, ranch, and vineyards. His granddaughter bequeathed the property to the nation.

THE STEVENSON HOUSE

530 Houston Street, Monterey. (408) 649-2836. Tours every hour on the hour, 10–4. Adult state parks ticket, $1, usable at all state parks that day.

Robert Louis Stevenson spent a few months in a second-floor room of this boardinghouse during 1879. He had traveled from Scotland to visit Fanny Osbourne, who later became his wife. He wrote *The Old Pacific Capital* here and the house, restored to look as it did then, is filled with Stevenson memorabilia. The lovely garden makes a nice waiting room for the hourly tour.

COLTON HALL MUSEUM OF THE CITY OF MONTEREY

Dutra and King Streets, Monterey. (408) 646-3851. Daily 10–5. Free.

Colton Hall, the first town hall and public school of Monterey, is famed as the site, in 1849, of the first Constitutional Congress of the new State of California. Here, the California Constitution was written in Spanish and English and the Great Seal of the state was designed. The large meeting room is furnished as it was then, with biographies and portraits of each of the men who signed the constitution, including Larkin, Vallejo, Ellis, Sutter, and Ord. A twenty-six-star flag flies.

Behind Colton Hall is the old *Monterey Jail,* open daily until 4:30. The walls are thick stone, the doors iron, and the cells pitch black and scary. It is impossible to believe that this was used as the city jail until May, 1959, but that's what the sign says.

THE CUSTOM HOUSE

1 Custom House Plaza, 115 Alvarado Street, Monterey. (408) 649-2836. Daily 10–5. $1.

The United States flag was first officially raised in California on this roof in 1846. Today, you walk into a long room that holds the exact duplicate of the cargo Richard Henry Dana wrote about in his *Two Years Before the Mast.* There are casks of liquor, cases of dishes, bags of nails, coffee, flour, and wagon wheels. A screeching yellow and green parrot lords over ribbons, ropes, cloth, soap, paper, tools, and trunks. In one corner are piles of "California bank notes"—the cowhides used for trading. The Custom House manager's quarters upstairs features a comfortable carved bed and chest, a table and a desk with an open book, and a cigar ready to be lit.

PACIFIC HOUSE

8 Custom House Plaza, Monterey. (408) 649-2837. Daily 10–5. Adult state parks ticket, $1.

The first floor of this tavern-court-newspaper-church-ballroom is now a museum of California history with artifact-filled cases arranged chronologically, beginning with the Costanoan Indians. Spanish saddles and money, gold miners' tools, a whaling boat, and the Victorian furniture of the pioneers are all here.

Upstairs is the Holman Collection, a remarkable gathering of Indian relics from all over North America. Costanoan religion, hunting, fishing, gathering, and processing of acorns, housing, trade, warfare, transportation, and survival lessons are explained with artifacts and models. Visitors can compare the arrows, games, beads, and baskets of many tribes, from Alaskan Eskimos to American Indians.

CASA DEL ORO

Scott and Olivier Streets, Monterey. (408) 649-2836. Daily 10–5. Free.

Thomas Larkin built this trading store in 1845. During the Gold Rush, when the big iron safe stored the miners' gold, the building became known as The House of Gold. Visitors can stand at the door to look at this fully equipped general store of the last century. Sewing machines and furniture are piled high, with chairs hanging from the rafters. Bags of coffee, bolts of cloth, cans of milk, and barrels of food all wait for customers. Located between the Pacific Building and the First Theater, Casa del Oro offers a few interesting moments.

CALIFORNIA'S FIRST THEATER

Scott and Pacific Streets, Monterey. (408) 649-2836. 9–5 except Monday and Tuesday. Box office: Wednesday–Sunday, 1–8; 375-4916. Adult ticket, $1, usable at all state buildings that day.

Jack Swan's lodging house gave its first performance of a stage play in 1847 to entertain bored soldiers. Since then, theatrical productions have been produced regularly and now nineteenth-century melodramas are performed on weekends. During the day, a ranger shows you through the theater and tells you about what you'd like to know. He'll tell you that they used to serve hot peanuts until the villain of the plays complained about being hit, that Lola Montez visited Monterey (and why), and where Swan got his 1800 hurdy-gurdy. Several present-day movie heroes made their acting debuts here with the Troupers of the Gold Coast. If you look carefully, you can spot them on recent billboards.

Two new buildings have just been made available to the public on the block next to the First Theater. The Old Whaling Station, located between Pacific Street and Custom House Plaza, was modeled after the owner's 1840 Scots home. As headquarters for Portuguese whalers in the 1850s, the beach was soon known for the whale oil rendering. A whalebone walk in front of the house is a reminder of those days. The First Brick House was built by Gallant G. Dickenson, who fired his own bricks in 1846, prospered in the gold country, and served as a delegate to the California Constitutional Convention. Both buildings are part of California's State Parks Department.

CASA SOBRANES

Pacific and Del Monte, Monterey. (408) 649-2836. Friday–Wednesday, tours on the hour from 9 to 4. Adult state parks ticket, $1.

"The House with the Blue Gate" is a little-changed typical home of Mexican California. Its style is Mediterranean with gracious, simple furnishings.

U.S. ARMY MUSEUM

The Presidio, Monterey. (408) 242-8414. Thursday–Monday, 9–12:30 and 1:30–4. Free.

This Army-run museum displays the history of old Fort Hill from the Ohlone Indian period to the present. Monuments to Commander John Drake Sloat and Father Junipero Serra adjoin the museum. Ten history sites are located nearby: Rumsen village sites and ceremonial rock, Father Serra's landing place, and the ruins of the first American fort in Monterey. The museum collection includes uniforms from the turn of the century, saddles, swords, sabers and other army equipment, and dioramas of early forts and the first Presidio.

PACIFIC GROVE MUSEUM OF NATURAL HISTORY

Forest and Central Avenues, Pacific Grove. (408) 372-4212. Daily except Monday, 10–5. Free.

Each October, thousands of Monarch butterflies arrive in Pacific Grove to winter in a grove of pine trees until March. Visitors who arrive in other months, and don't want to climb a pine tree, can see a marvelous exhibit of the Monarch in this museum. There is also a large collection of tropical and other California butterflies, as well as sea otters; fish; mammals; rodents; insects; and birds, stuffed and in photos. The skeleton of a sea otter playing with a clamshell is particularly touching.

The nearby Bear Flag Museum, 599 Lighthouse Avenue, houses historical artifacts and interesting memorabilia.

POINT PIÑOS LIGHTHOUSE

Off Seventeen-Mile Drive, Pacific Grove. (408) 373-3304. Weekends in summer, 1–4. Free.

The oldest lighthouse (1855) on the West Coast, Point Piños overlooks the meadows and sand dunes of a golf course on one side and a white-capped ocean on the other. A small U.S. Coast Guard maritime museum is open to the public upstairs, and downstairs a modern computer-operated signal is sent out to fog-bound ships.

Nearby, on the way into town, Lovers Point offers marine gardens, a small rocky beach, tree-shaded picnic grounds, and glass-bottomed boats in summer.

MISSION SAN CARLOS BORROMEO

Rio Road off Highway 1, Carmel. (408) 624-3600. Monday–Saturday 9:30–4:30; Sundays and holidays, 10:30–4:30. Donation.

This lovely mission church and cemetery, two museums, and the adobe home of the pioneer Munras family combine to make this mission a "must stop." Father Junipero Serra rests in the church and in the cemetery lies Old Gabriel, 151 years old, baptized by Father Serra. A small museum in the garden houses pictures of the original mission and its restoration. There are Indian grinding pots, arrowheads, baskets, beads, toys, and two Indian skeletons buried with eagle claws and turtles. The long main museum offers fine art from the original mission and a replica of the stark cell Father Serra died in. You'll also find California's first library here—Father Serra's books, bibles, theologies, sermons, travel commentaries, lives of the saints, and technical works. Altar pieces, saddles, the furnished kitchen and dining room, and some of the mission priests' vestments are here, too.

The *Casa Munras* is now a memorial to the Munras family. There are keys from the original adobe, embroidery, family pictures, music and provision boxes, jewelry, maps, chocolate pots, and dresses. The Munras living room is furnished with a cradle and doll buggy, Victorian ornaments, a marble fireplace, and handsome carved furniture.

POINT LOBOS STATE RESERVE

Route 1, south of Carmel. (408) 624-4909. Daily 9–5 in winter, later in summer. Cars, $2.

Early Spanish explorers named this rocky, surf-swept point of land "Punta de Los Lobos Marinos," or Point of the Sea Wolves. You can still hear the loud barking of the sea lions and see them on offshore rocks. Point Lobos is an outdoor museum: Each tree, plant, and shrub is protected by law, as are the cormorants, pelicans, otters, squirrels, and black-tailed mule deer that live here. One of the last natural stands of Monterey cypress is also found at the reserve. Picnics are allowed in designated areas and there are seven miles of hiking trails.

CARMEL

A visit to the Monterey Peninsula is not complete without an hour or two of browsing in the picturesque village of Carmel. The Pine Inn Block, bounded by Ocean Avenue, Lincoln, Monte Verde, and Sixth Avenue is an ever-changing scene of Victorian shops, gardens, and restaurants. Of special interest to the children: Sylvia's Danish Pastry Shop (Sixth and Dolores; (408) 624-1198) for creamy goodies; the Gallery of Fine Comic Art (Seventh and Mission, 624-3278); and Thinker Toys (Carmel Plaza; 9–9 daily; Sunday 10–5:30) for a den of games, educational and imported toys, puppets and dollhouse furnishings. The Mediterranean Market at Ocean and Mission supplies picnic items for your walk on Carmel Beach, at the end of Ocean Avenue, one of the most beautiful on the coast.

The Steinbeck House

THUNDERBIRD BOOK SHOP AND RESTAURANT

The Barnyard, Carmel Valley. (408) 624-1803. Summer, 10–9:30; winter, 10–5:30 weekdays; Sunday, 11–5.

The Thunderbird is just what you dream a bookstore might be—a place where browsing is welcomed and the selection of books for children and adults is phenomenal. One corner of the store is a restaurant, serving lunch every day and dinner Tuesday through Sunday.

THE STEINBECK HOUSE

132 Central Avenue, Salinas. (408) 757-3106. Tours by appointment. Lunch reservations: 424-2735.

John Steinbeck's childhood Victorian home is now a luncheon restaurant with seatings at 11:45 or 1:15, Monday through Friday. The refurbished home offers fresh produce of the valley amid Steinbeck memorabilia. Profits go to various charities in the Salinas Valley.

The *Steinbeck Library*, at 110 West San Luis, (408) 758-7311, displays an extensive collection of John Steinbeck's memorabilia, including reviews and personal correspondence and a lifesize bronze statue.

ISSEI PIONEER MUSEUM

14 California Street, Salinas. (408) 424-4105. By appointment only.
The first and only Issei pioneer museum in the United States, housed in the annex of the Buddhist Temple, contains over six hundred items donated by Issei (first generation of Japanese to emigrate to the United States) and their descendants. Many of the articles were handmade by the Issei during World War II in Arizona and California relocation camps. The oldest item is a book about Tokyo, printed in 1850.

MISSION NUESTRA SEÑORA DE SOLEDAD

Soledad, Highway 101. (408) 678-2586. 10–4 except Tuesday. Free.
Founded in 1791, Soledad is partially restored. It's now a lovely oasis in a wind-swept valley. Visitors can visit the museum and chapel and then spend time in the gift shop, graveyard, and picnic area.

PINNACLES NATIONAL MONUMENT

Off Highway 101 at King City. (408) 389-4578. $1 per car per day.
Entered from Soledad or King City, Pinnacles National Monument is a little-known land of striking beauty. Its 14,000 acres are comparable in rock formations and color striations only to the Grand Canyon. The fern glens, caves, wild animals, and the curious pinnacles themselves, some rising 1,200 feet above the canyon floors, make this a perfect hiking spot in spring and fall.

SAN ANTONIO DE PADUA MISSION

Jolon, off Highway 101 from King City. (408) 385-4478. Daily 9–4:30. Donation.
In its Valley of the Oaks, San Antonio de Padua is one of the most interesting of the California missions. It still functions as a working mission, with olive and vine presses, fields planted and stock roaming the hills, just as it did in 1771, but on a much smaller scale. Inside the mission museum, you can walk through the candle- and soap-making rooms, visit a sample mission bedroom and the kitchens, and climb up to the original wine vat. Unfortunately, vandals have destroyed the beehive ovens, Temescal sweat houses, and aqueduct system once on the grounds. Steinbeck described the mission—abandoned during a drought—in *To a God Unknown*.

PUBLIC RELATIONS TOURS

CHAMPION INTERNATIONAL CORPORATION. *1078 Merrill, Salinas. (408) 424-1831. November–April, by appointment for children over 10.*
Visitors see manufacturing of corrugated boxes and paper laminations.

MONTEREY PENINSULA HERALD NEWSPAPER. *Pacific and Jefferson Streets, Monterey. (408) 372-3311. Tours by appointment.*

SALINAS CALIFORNIAN NEWSPAPER. *123 West Alisal, Salinas. (408) 424-2221 ext. 70. Tours by appointment.* Visitors will see "Big Red" print 56,000 newspapers per hour and editors, writers, and typesetters gathering news, producing, and printing the newspaper.

THE EAST BAY—ALAMEDA AND CONTRA COSTA COUNTIES

The East Bay, ranging along the east shore of San Francisco Bay, is a green land dotted with public parks and streams and crowned by Mt. Diablo. The places of interest in this area are some distance from each other, so it's advisable to plan ahead. The Berkeley hills across the bay from San Francisco and the Carquinez Straits frame the East Bay beautifully. Boaters, fishermen, picnickers, hikers, and nature lovers of all ages will find special places to visit here.

TREASURE ISLAND MUSEUM

Building 1, Treasure Island. (415) 765-6182. Daily 10–3:30. Free.

Exhibits interpret the history of the Navy, Marine Corps, and Coast Guard in the Pacific and the Treasure Island World's Fair of 1939–40. Artifacts include the Farallon Islands Lighthouse lens, a 1920 diver's suit, ship models, weapons, and curious World's Fair mementos.

JACK LONDON SQUARE

Foot of Broadway, Oakland.

Busy waterfront stores and restaurants and a constantly changing view of ships in the Oakland estuary make Jack London Square an interesting place for children to stroll around. At one end of the square is a special treasure—the Jack London Klondike Cabin, a small sod-covered cabin that housed Jack London in Yukon Territory during the Gold Rush in 1897. You'll see the crude furniture, rusty stove, shovels, snowshoes, gas lamps, pots, and traps that Jack London used. The First and Last Chance saloon— in which Jack London is said to have imbibed—is nearby.

The Bret Harte Boardwalk a few blocks away is a pretty row of shops restored to their 1880s splendor.

THE GINGERBREAD HOUSE

741 Fifth Street, between Brush and Castro, Oakland. (415) 444-7373. Tuesday–

Thursday, 11–6; Friday and Saturday, 11–7:30. Reserve for lunch or dinner.

Hansel and Gretel's wicked witch would be envious of this tasty-looking shop and restaurant. Inside you'll find gingerbread cookies, puppets, dolls, aprons, potholders, cards, T-shirts—even gingerbread bubble bath. There's also a Black history collection and T. J. Robinson's old doll collection. Jambalaya, creole, and cornbread are some of the Southern favorites served in the restaurant.

EAST BAY NEGRO HISTORICAL SOCIETY

4519 Grove, Oakland. (415) 658-3158. Tuesday, 12:30–7; Wednesday–Friday, 12:30–5:30; and by appointment. Free.

California's Black Americans and their history is the theme of this lovingly put-together, information-crammed collection. The collection focuses on individual families, such as the William Sugg family of Sonora—the donor's grandfather's freedom papers are framed on the wall; his grandmother was born in a covered wagon on the way to Gold Country in 1851 (their gold mining pan and a doll buggy from their house are there, too)—but Black American athletes, musicians, scientists, and politicians are remembered, too. The three Black miners who struck it rich and gave money for the Mt. Oliver Baptist Church in Marysville are remembered. So are the cowboys and farmers and doctors who are the forebears of Ruth Lasartemay who runs the museum. William Leidesdorff, treasurer of the town of San Francisco; James Beckworth, noted scout and explorer; Pio Pico, area founding father; and Colonel Allensworth, who founded a town near Fresno are all noted. Our favorite item is the christening dress of the child born to a lady-in-waiting to Queen Victoria who'd run off to the West Indies with the Black coachman and then settled in San Francisco.

DUNSMUIR HOUSE AND GARDEN

2960 Peralta Oaks Court, 106 Avenue exit on Highway 580. (415) 562-7588. May–October, Sunday and Wednesday, 12–4. Opens its Christmas display Thanksgiving week. House tour, adults, $3; children and seniors, $2; garden tour, $1.

If you'd like to see the movie set for "Burnt Offerings," and perhaps future Gothics, this is the place—it's just missing a few cobwebs. The stained glass domed roof and the music room are remarkable.

The nearby Moss Cottage (Mosswood Park), built in the mid-1800s, is a rare example of Gothic Revival Victorian, with arches, gables, spires, stained glass, and gingerbread echoing memories of days gone by.

THE OAKLAND MUSEUM

1000 Oak Street, Oakland. (415) 273-3401. Wednesday–Saturday, 10–5; Sunday, 12–7. Free.

The Oakland Museum is three first-rate museums in one: California art,

California history, and California natural sciences. You can always be sure of finding an afternoon's worth of interesting things for children of all ages.

The top level concentrates on California art from the days of the Spanish explorers to the present. Panoramic views of San Francisco, cowboys and Indians, Asian art found in California homes, and modern canvases are all intriguing.

The natural sciences level includes exhibits on botany, birds, ecology, paleontology, and geology. An aquarium with everything from turkey fish to seahorses, and dioramas of mammals, birds, rodents, and snakes in their natural settings provide fascinating models of the real thing.

The California history level is perhaps the best of all. Begin with the Indians here in 3000 B.C. and walk through "rooms" of the state's history, from the Spanish explorers, the Californios, to the gold miners and wild west cowboys, to the pioneers and turn-of-the-century Californians. The pioneer kitchen, with one chair of those grouped around the table actually outside the glass, so the young visitor can pretend he's in the kitchen, is one thing we always head for.

Concerts, films, and special exhibits on man and nature are scheduled regularly and the snack bar is open until 3:30.

The Oakland Museum

CAMRON-STANFORD HOUSE

1418 Lakeside Drive, Oakland. (415) 836-1976. Wednesday, 11–4; Sunday, 1–5. Free.

This 1876 Italianate-style Victorian provides a look at Oakland history since the days of the horse cars and gas lighting, when Lake Merritt was not a lake. Four rooms are furnished to reflect the local style of the Victorian era. Multimedia shows and special exhibits, and curators who point out the wooden columns made to look like stone and the furbelows and curlicues produced by machine add to the young visitor's enjoyment.

LAKESIDE PARK

Off Grand Avenue, Lake Merritt, Oakland. (415) 273-3091. 9–5 daily.

A narrow strip of grass around Lake Merritt offers peace in the center of a busy city. In the Kiwanis Kiddie Korner, children can slide down an octopus or swing on a sea horse.

The Rotary Natural Science Center (10–5 daily, 273-3739) shows free nature films on occasion, in addition to its regular fare of science exhibits and an aviary and zoo holding turkey vultures, barn owls, great horned owls, hawks, and sand-hill cranes, as well as possums, porcupines, and skunks. This is the oldest wildlife refuge in the United States and for 15¢ you can buy duck food to feed the free-flying waterfowl, which includes an occasional pelican.

Sailboats, houseboats, and paddleboats are offered for rent. *The Merritt Queen*, a replica of a Mississippi river boat, takes half-hour tours of the lake (50¢ for adults, 35¢ for children and seniors) during summer vacations and on weekends.

The Lakeside Toy Train runs from 12:30–5:30 on weekends, depending on business. The round trip to Fairyland is 25¢ and takes fifteen minutes.

CHILDREN'S FAIRYLAND

Lakeside Park, Oakland. (415) 452-2259. Wednesday–Sunday, 10–4:30. Adults, $1.50; children, 10¢.

Duck through Mother Goose's Shoe to meet Alice, the Cheshire Cat, the Cowardly Lion, and the Queen of Fairyland. Then slide down a dragon's back, or sail on a pea green boat with the Owl and the Pussycat. Pinocchio, Willie the Whale, slides, mazes, rides, and enchanted bowers come to life. All of the characters in Fairyland are here to make children smile and a magic key unlocks their stories ($1). The Wonder-Go-Round and Magic Web Ferris wheel are nominally priced; puppet shows and clown shows are free.

OAKLAND ZOO AND BABY ZOO

Knowland State Park, MacArthur Freeway at Golf Links Road and Ninety-eighth

Avenue, Oakland. (415) 632-9523. 10–4 daily. $3 per car and $6 per bus. Rides are 50¢ and $1 (special value ticket books are available). Admission to the Baby Zoo is $1 for adults, 75¢ for children. Group rates and tours available.

This beautifully arranged zoo is one of the nicest in the state. Glide over the African Veldt and up into the hills on the 1250-foot Skyfari Ride or take a miniature train for a breathtaking view of the bay. At the Baby Zoo you can pet and feed a variety of friendly animals. Be sure to see the elephant show on weekends. Picnic, barbecue, and playground facilities are located throughout the park.

McCONAGHY ESTATE

18701 Hesperian Boulevard, Hayward. (415) 276-3010. Thursday–Sunday, 1–4 and by appointment. (278-0198). Adults, $2; seniors, $1.50; children 6–12, 50¢; classes, $5. Special Christmas program.

This elegant 1886 farmhouse is so completely furnished it looks as if the family still lives there. One bedroom is filled with toys, games, books, and clothes used by the turn-of-the-century child. The kitchen displays an ice box, wood stove, and a pump. The dining room is lavishly decorated for each holiday. A tank house and a buggy-filled carriage house adjoin the house, handily located next to Kennedy Park with its picnic tables, merry-go-round, and train.

CHABOT OBSERVATORY AND PLANETARIUM

4917 Mountain Boulevard, near MacArthur Freeway and Warren Boulevard, Oakland. (415) 531-4560. Friday and Saturday, 7:30 p.m. Children's program Saturday at 1. Adults, $1.50; children, 50¢. Reservations advised.

The changing two-hour show here includes a movie, science demonstration, and the planetarium program. A recent show presented an exciting space voyage. Youngsters learn how astronomers explore the universe and get a chance to observe the planets and stars through a telescope. Locating the Big and Little Dippers during the planetarium show is always a popular part of the program.

SULPHUR CREEK PARK

1801 D Street, Hayward. (415) 881-6747. Monday–Saturday, 10–5; Sunday, 12–5. Free. Special tours and field trips.

Sulphur Creek Park is a charming, out-of-the-way spot in which to introduce children to nature. Wildlife native to Northern California and the Bay Area are kept at Sulphur Creek. Coyotes, raccoons, opossums, skunks, hawks, owls, song and garden birds, a variety of reptiles and amphibians, and invertebrates are displayed in naturalistic habitats. Hands-on exhibits range from studies of habitats to smells in nature and most exhibits change regularly. Local children can take advantage of the animal lending library to take home hamsters, rats, mice, rabbits, and guinea pigs.

HAYWARD AREA HISTORICAL SOCIETY MUSEUM

22701 Main, at C, Hayward. (415) 581-0223. Monday–Saturday, 12–4. Free.

The large brick 1927 post office is now a lovingly presented album of Hayward history. Ladies' derringers and antique guns, cameras, dolls, baby buggies, teddybears, scrapbooks full of high school pictures, tax records and family albums, one thousand handkerchiefs, a stereopticon, a 1923 fire engine, an 1820s hand-drawn fire pumper that was shipped around the Horn to San Francisco in 1849, doctors' and midwives' instruments, and post office, fire, police, and veterans displays are a little overwhelming. The gracious curator enjoys playing the old phonographs for youngsters and telling them the stories behind these artifacts.

MISSION SAN JOSE

43300 Mission Boulevard, Fremont. (415) 657-1797. Daily, 10–4:30 in winter; until 5 in summer. Donation.

Founded in 1797, Mission San Jose has had an exciting place in California history. A highlight of the museum tour is an exhibit demonstrating the history and culture of the Ohlone, the native people of the Bay Area. Father Duran, who arrived in 1806, taught some of the two thousand Ohlone neophytes to play the original mission bells and musical instruments now on display. Vestments worn by Father Serra, timbers and rawhides from the original mission building, an 1890s buggy, the original baptismal font, a pioneer cradle, and the sanctus bells are housed in the adobe living quarters of the mission padres. The mission church has been carefully reconstructed from hand-hewn beams and over 180,000 adobe blocks.

REFUGE HEADQUARTERS INTERPRETIVE CENTER

Highway 84, near Dumbarton Bridge toll plaza, Fremont. (415) 792-3178. Wednesday–Sunday, 10–5. Free.

Photographic exhibits on special environmental programs, nature study walks, slide and film programs and self-guided walks through the salt marsh and diked ponds at Newark Slough help introduce youngsters to the world around them.

AMADOR-LIVERMORE VALLEY MUSEUM

603 Main Street, Pleasanton. (415) 462-2766. Wednesday–Friday, 1–4 and by appointment. Free.

This new museum features both platform exhibits such as a blacksmith shop, a 1930s beauty parlor, and a one-room school, as well as changing panel exhibits on historical topics.

History buffs may want to visit the Dublin Heritage Center in the Old Murray School (6600 Donlon Way, 828-3377) now in the process of being restored.

LIVERMORE HISTORY CENTER

2155 Third Street, Livermore. (415) 449-9927. Wednesday–Sunday, 11:30–4. Free.

This teaching exhibit of the history of the Livermore Valley from pre-historic times to the present is housed in the old Carnegie Library. Fossilized oysters, pictures, maps, and artifacts from the local coal mines and fuse factory are on display, along with a uniform used in the recent reenactment of the de Anza expedition. The museum members are currently working on the restoration of the Historical Highway Garage, in Livermore on North L and Portola, which will be a museum of local transportation.

Ravenswood, the Victorian cottage and gardens built by San Francisco's "Blind Boss" Buckley, is occasionally open to the public. (It's on Arroyo Road, call 447-7300 for an appointment.) Visitors may see cloisonné chandeliers, an ornate billiard table, clothing, pictures, and mementos of the Buckley family.

RICHMOND MUSEUM

400 Nevin, Richmond. (415) 235-7387. Saturday and Sunday, 1–4 and by appointment. Free.

Richmond residents from the days of the Native Americans up to 1945 are portrayed in the permanent history gallery of this bright new museum through dioramas and panel displays. Old-time vehicles such as a peddlers' wagon and an old fire engine are on the site. Kids will also enjoy the recreations of rooms and old stores as well as the changing exhibits, from antique toys to African artifacts.

UNIVERSITY ART MUSEUM

2626 Bancroft Way, Berkeley. (415) 642-1207. Wednesday–Sunday, 11–5. Adults, $2; senior citizens, $1.

Berkeley's museum is a natural for children, not so much for the art but for the building itself. Its unique multileveled, concrete-slab construction enables a young visitor to see its spacious interiors from any of the many corners and balconies. The outdoor sculpture garden is fun and the primitive art usually strikes a chord with young people.

The Pacific Film Archive, located in the museum basement (642-1412/1124) shows old and rare films every evening.

McCALLUM'S FAMOUS ICE CREAM

1825 Solano, Berkeley. (415) 525-3510. Daily 8 A.M.–11 P.M.; Friday and Saturday till midnight.

McCallum's specializes in delicious and mountainous ice cream creations. Try the hot fudge sundae, served with a pitcher of hot sauce on the side, or the toasted almond chocolate shake in a tall glass lined with fudge. The Large McCallum's Nightmare serves four to eight for $15 and $25. The

Sink, at $30, serves more—it has dozens of shovels of ice cream in many flavors and almost as many toppings. Everything is dished out by Scottish-garbed lads and lassies, and there are cones on the other side of the store for on-the-run tasting.

LAWRENCE HALL OF SCIENCE

Centennial Drive, University of California, Berkeley. (415) 642-5132; Monday–Friday, 10–4:30. Thursday evening until 9; Saturday and Sunday, 10–5. Adults,

Biology lab in the Lawrence Hall of Science

$2.50; students, seniors, and children 7–18, $1.50.

Our ten- and twelve-year-old nephews had to be dragged away from this place at closing time. There are almost too many exhibits—science workshops, tests of your mathematical and logical ability, tests of knowledge, computers to play with, visual oddities that help you learn more about how your eyes work, and a hundred different mechanical things to tantalize and amuse. The Biology Lab is the place to investigate the world of living things (open weekends, 1:30–4:30). There is also an extensive mineral and gem collection and a grand view of the bay, the bridges, and San Francisco. There are special exhibits on whales each winter, dinosaurs in spring, and robots in summer.

Budding botanists might want to visit the U.C. Botanical Lab in Strawberry Canyon to see cacti, orchids, and California plants (9–4:45 daily).

LOWIE MUSEUM

Kroeber Hall, University of California, Berkeley. (415) 642-3681. Monday, Tuesday, Thursday, Friday, 10–4:30; weekends, 1–4:30. Donation.

Across the street from the University Art Museum, a totem pole chronicles the family history of an Indian chief from the Queen Charlotte Islands and points the way to more archeological treasures. Permanent exhibits include photos of Ishi, things that Ishi made, and plaster casts of Pleistocene Man. "Life After Life" in Egypt is part of the rotating lifestyles and cultural exhibits.

THE CAMPANILE

Sather Tower, University of California, Berkeley. (415) 642-6000. Daily, 10–4:15. 25¢.

From the top of this tower, you can see San Francisco, Alcatraz, Mt. Tamalpais, the Golden Gate and Bay bridges, and the entire campus. Above you twelve bronze bells weighing almost nine tons ring out melodies three times a day and you see them being played.

HALL OF HEALTH

John Muir School, 2955 Claremont Avenue, Berkeley. (415) 549-1564/540-1364. School days, 10:15–3. Free. Groups by appointment.

Alta Bates Hospital has put together this entertaining yet educational collection of games, displays, and exhibits on health and the human body.

DIABLO VALLEY COLLEGE MUSEUM AND PLANETARIUM

321 Golf Club Road, Pleasant Hill. (415) 684-1230. Museum: Hours change each semester. Planetarium shows. Groups by appointment. 50¢.

In this museum youngsters can see a seismograph working, a Foucault pendulum swinging, and changing oceanography and anthropological exhibits on Native Americans. Local animals, especially the nocturnal moles, weasels, and owls are fun to see too.

TILDEN REGIONAL PARK & ENVIRONMENTAL EDUCATION CENTER

Canyon Drive off Grizzly Peak Boulevard, Berkeley. (415) 525-2233. Daily except Monday, 10–5. Little Farm, daily, 8–5. Free. Rides are nominally priced.

Tilden Park has a pony ride, a historic merry-go-round, a duck pond, and a miniature train. Botanical gardens, a nature center, and swimming in Lake Anza are some of the other recreational facilities in this well-equipped park. But the chief attraction, especially for young people, is the Little Farm. Mary Ann the Mexican burro, Snuffy the sheep, Rosebud the pig, and Buttercup the cow are among the family members of this charming little farm. There are chickens, ducks, and rabbits to feed and pet as well. Children are taught to walk toward the animals for petting and how to feed them—with a flattened hand and only the foods that are good for them.

ALEXANDER LINDSAY JUNIOR MUSEUM

1901 First Avenue, Walnut Creek. (415) 935-1978. School year: Wednesday–Friday, 1–5; weekends, 12–4. Summer: Wednesday–Sunday, 11–5. Free.

A collection of native wild animals close enough to touch; aquariums of native fish and amphibians; and a collection of rocks, fossils, shells, and Indian artifacts are the main features of this small museum, which specializes in caring for and rehabilitating wounded birds of prey and other wild animals. Foxes, owls, hawks, raccoons, vultures, opossums, boas, and King snakes are a few of the animals on display. Rabbits, rats, hamsters, and guinea pigs can be rented.

History buffs will want to visit Shadelands Ranch Historical Museum, 2660 Ygnacio Valley Road, Walnut Creek, (415) 935-7871, 1–4 Wednesday–Sunday, closed August.

BLACK DIAMOND MINE REGIONAL PRESERVE

Follow Highway 4 to Somersville Road, head south to road's end, Antioch. (415) 757-2620. 8 A.M. to dusk daily. By reservation. Parking, $2.

One-and-a-half- and two-and-a-half-hour tours take you down into a coal mine to see veins of coal and to learn about mining and area history. Then you hike up to a legend-filled graveyard.

JOHN MUIR NATIONAL HISTORIC SITE

4202 Alhambra Avenue, Martinez. (415) 228-8860. Tours on weekend afternoons and by appointment. Film shown throughout the day; house is open 8:30–4:30. Donation, ages 16–62.

After a beautiful half-hour film narrated from John Muir's text and scenes of the natural wonders that inspired it, visitors go through Muir's large nineteenth-century farmhouse, which is one of the most authentically presented houses you can visit. Details such as closets filled with clothing; Muir's suitcase on the bed ready for travel; and the glasses and pencils, books and papers standing ready on Muir's desk in his "scribble den," give the house a lived-in look. You can go up to the treasure-filled attic and ring the ranch bell in the bell tower.

The Little Farm at Tilden Regional Park

Also on the Muir property is the *Martinez Adobe*, which was built by the son of the Mexican don whose family built the town of Martinez. The thick-walled adobe has served as headquarters for the Rancho foreman's quarters on the Muir Ranch, and as the home of Muir's daughter and family. You may wander through the grounds to look at the exotic plants Muir gathered and stay as long as you like. Birdwalks and Junior Ranger programs on selected Saturdays.

BENICIA CAPITOL STATE HISTORIC PARK

First and G Streets, Benicia. (707) 745-3385. Daily 10–5. Adult ticket, 25¢, usable at all state parks that day.

Benicia was the capital of California for over a year, and the capitol building looks now as it did in 1854. The exhibit room provides the history of early California. Our fourth graders were fascinated with the whale oil lamps, quill pens, and shiny brass cuspidors.

Across the colorful garden is the Fischer-Hanlon House (weekends, 12–4 and by appointment. 745-1554), a proper, upper-class merchant's home of the 1880s.

MURIEL'S DOLL HOUSE MUSEUM

33 Canyon Lake Drive, Port Costa. (415) 787-2820. Daily except Monday, 10–7 and by appointment. Adults, $1; children, 25¢.

Muriel herself greets you at the door. After you sign her guest book, you may browse through her assemblage of over 3,000 china, bisque, Parian, wood, wax, apple, tin, celluloid, and fashion dolls reflecting the customs and costumes of their respective eras. There are Indian dolls; Eskimo dolls; Amish dolls; Black dolls; and cornhusk, papier-mâché, and rag dolls. The shadow box scenes of an 1886 moonshiner's still, a 1900 barber shop, and the replica of Muriel's childhood home are fascinating. Muriel enjoys sharing the stories about her dolls and makes the visit most enjoyable.

THE ALVARADO ADOBE AND BLUME HOUSE MUSEUM

1 Alvarado Square, San Pablo. (415) 236-7373. Weekends 1–5, and by appointment.

The Alvarado Adobe has been precisely reconstructed on its original site. The owner, Juan Bautista Alvarado, husband of Martina Castro, was the Mexican governor of California in 1840 and lived here until 1882. (The house itself was built in the early 1840s for the Castro family.) Although it's still in the process of being furnished in a mix of Rancho and Early California styles, visitors can see showcases of Indian artifacts found in local Indian mounds, *cascarone* balls—painted egg shells that had been filled with confetti or cologne with which to hit fellow party-goers, an Indian shell game, and samples of the soap plant—*amole*—which was roasted and eaten; boiled for glue; pounded into a paste which stupefied fish when thrown into a stream;

used for twine, shampoo, and soap; and dried to stuff mattresses.

The Blume Museum is a 1920s farmhouse now refurnished to look as it did then, with oak furniture, early plumbing fixtures, and an iron stove in the kitchen.

PUBLIC RELATIONS TOURS

RICHMOND REFINERY TOURS. *Chevron's Richmond Refinery and Research Facilities. (415) 894-4940.* Tours for high school, college, and community groups by appointment.

HERMAN GOELITZ CANDY CO. *947 61st Street, Oakland. (415) 652-2168. By appointment.* See how jelly bellies and jelly beans are made.

THE CHEESE FACTORY. *830 Main Street, Oakland. (415) 846-2577. Daily, 9–6. Groups by appointment.* Watch cheese manufacturing and have free tastes.

PARAMOUNT THEATRE OF THE ARTS. *2025 Broadway, Oakland. (415) 893-2300. Tours first and third Saturday of each month, 10 A.M. $1 per person. Children under 10 not advisable. By appointment.* The Paramount, which has regular programs of interest to children, is the best example of Art Deco architecture on the West Coast. Parquet floors, a gold ceiling teeming with sculptured life, and elegant embellishments almost compete with what's on stage.

GIM SHING BAKERY/DBA FORTUNE COOKIE FACTORY. *263 Twelfth Street, Oakland. (415) 832-5552. Monday–Saturday, 10–3 and by appointment. Groups, 75 ¢ per person (everyone gets a bag of cookies).*

SACRAMENTO AND STOCKTON AREA

The Sacramento Area is the political heartland of the state of California. Two hours away from San Francisco, the city of Sacramento is worth a visit to see how the state functions—from the legislative rooms and state displays in the Capitol to the judicial buildings in Capitol Square. The state capital of California has been in Benicia, Vallejo, and San Jose. Now, after the one hundredth anniversary of the Capitol building in 1979 and the restoration of the dome, Sacramento seems to be the permanent capital of the State. The green farmland surrounding the city is reflected in the forty-acre Capitol Park within the city, and visitors will appreciate the combination of rural and urban surroundings.

Stockton, south of Sacramento, is the entrance to the Gold Country. Visitors will find the rolling hills and good green farmland dotted by pleasant towns and villages. Stockton is named in honor of Commodore Robert Stockton, who led the forces which took over California for the United States in 1847.

The lakes and peacefulness of the San Joaquin Valley add to the ambience of the area—and water-sports lovers will find ample space for houseboating, skiing, fishing, and every kind of boating.

THE NUT TREE

Monte Vista Avenue, off Highway 80, Vacaville. (707) 448-6411. Daily, 7 A.M.–9 P.M.

The highway signs for the Nut Tree are so pretty you wonder if the restaurant can live up to them. It does. The Nut Tree is much more than a restaurant—it's an afternoon (or morning) of enjoyment. In the restaurant itself, three lavishly decorated rooms face huge glass aviaries where brilliantly colored birds fly, sing, and eat fruits and seeds. The lunch menu includes salads, sandwiches, and special lunches priced from $6. Every dinner comes with an individual loaf of warm bread. Prices are higher at dinner, but you can still order a Dutch plate of cold meats and cheese or a splendiferous fresh fruit plate. Beer is imported from nine countries and the desserts are divine. Children under ten rate a special Train Rider's menu. In the shopping area, a cheese and beer bar is comfortable and there are snack bars outside. Free mechanical animals, play mirrors, Polynesian tree huts and a funny face play wall will entice the children for hours. Outside the toy store, they can board a miniature train for a five-minute ride ($1 each, three for $2.50). Just think, all this sprang from a single walnut planted by a twelve-year-old girl in 1860.

The Nut Tree

VACAVILLE MUSEUM

213 Buck Avenue, Vacaville. (707) 447-4513. Wednesday–Sunday, 1–4:30. Adults, $1; students, 50¢; Wednesday free to all.

This pleasant new museum honors the city's heritage, its founders and its ancestors, and the farmers who have settled Solano County. Rotating exhibits such as the Vaca Valley Doll Club's collection and kitchenware of the twenties and thirties are of interest to the whole family.

The nearby Peña Adobe, on Highway 80 five miles south of Vacaville, is open during the day for visitors who want to see what rancho life was really like. The Peña Adobe is the original one, built on an ancient Indian site, and some of the Wintu artifacts found during restoration are shown. There are picnic tables on the grounds.

VAC-AERO

Peña Adobe exit, Highway 80. 10 A.M. to sunset, weather permitting. (707) 447-4500. Gliding and flying rides and lessons. P.O. Box 176, Vacaville, 95688.

Gliding flights last about fifteen glorious silent minutes or you can go up for a scenic cruise in a 1928 Travelaire biplane or the more spectacular , aerobatic ride in the Great Lakes replica biplane.

Other soaring centers in Northern California are:
Ames Soaring Club, Patterson Pass Road, Livermore. (415) 447-4110.
Bay Area Soaring Association, 2728 Oak Road, Walnut Creek. (415) 356-9576/984-3045.
Big Valley Soaring, 12145 De Vries Road, Lodi. (209) 466-9820.
Chico Soaring Association, Chico Municipal Airport. (916) 342-6599.
Donner Aviation, Truckee Airport. (916) 587-6559.
North Bay Soaring Club, Sonoma Skypark, San Rafael. (707) 644-0109.
Sacramento Soaring Club, Truckee Airport. (916) 961-8854.
Sky Sailing Airport, Christy Street, Fremont. (415) 651-7671.
Soaring Experience, Inc., Same address as above. (415) 569-2404.
East Bay Soaring Club, 441 San Carlos Way, Novato. (415) 897-4792.

SUTTER'S FORT AND STATE INDIAN MUSEUM STATE HISTORIC PARK

2701 L Street, Sacramento. (916) 445-4209. Daily except holidays, 10–5. Adults, $1 (including information wand); under 18, 50¢ (with information wands). Tickets usable at all state historic parks that day.

Sutter's Fort is one of the best places to relive California history. The fort and its buildings and stables are perfectly reconstructed and the cooperage, distillery, saddle shop, candle-making room, kitchens, trading post, Indian guard room, *vaqueros'* bunk room, and Sutter's bachelor and family quarters are all as they once were. The songs and information provided through the wands are clear, helpful, and entertaining. While facing a model of James Marshall showing Sutter the gold he found at the mill, you hear their conversation and Sutter's German-Swiss accent. A pioneer lady talks to herself as she bends over the stove, Indians sing while working at shuttle and loom. Live sheep still stand in the stables and the fire still glows in the black-smith shop. A small museum relates Sutter's biography and the life of the California pioneers. Our kids were especially taken with the diorama of John Fremont and Kit Carson entering the fort in 1844. The doll that survived the Donner party is also special.

Next to Sutter's Fort, the *State Indian Museum* (2618 K Street, same hours and phone) houses a fine collection of California Indian relics. The exhibits span archaeology, basketry, featherwork, pottery, maps, minerals, musical in-struments, clothing, ceremonies, boats, housing, and jewelry. Did you know that there were over 750 languages spoken by the Indians of North Amer-ica? Do you know the tribes of Northern California? Here you'll see Maidus grinding acorns, a Mono storage shelter, a Pomo tule boat, a Miwok head-dress, a Yokuts dice game, and the ghost dance of the Sioux and Cheyenne. Ishi, last of his California tribe, is here in photographs, starting a fire, skin-ning a deer, painting, carving, sewing. Other civilizations were here before we were; this place makes you aware of how little we know of them. Children can start fires with a bow stick, grind corn, and feel animal fur. Youngsters can have lessons in wool-making or basket weaving and groups can "live" on the fort for 24 hours, by appointment.

CALIFORNIA STATE CAPITOL

Capitol Mall, Sacramento. (916) 445-5200. Free tours from the East Entrance, Monday–Friday at 10:30, 1:30, 2:30, and by appointment.

Visitors may look in on the Assembly and the Senate when the legisla-ture is in session. Fifty-eight displays, one for each county in the state, are on the ground floor of the East Wing. The governor's office is right on the main floor, so you may spot him or some other celebrities.

For a different look at the history of California, stop in at the nearby California State Archives (1020 O Street, (916) 445-4293, Monday–Friday, 8–5), to walk through a well-designed exhibit area showing historic docu-ments and pictures.

E. B. CROCKER ART MUSEUM

216 O Street, Sacramento. (916) 449-5423. Daily except Mondays and holidays, 10–5; Tuesday, 2–10 P.M. Free.

The oldest art museum in the West was built around 1873 to house the paintings and prints collected by Judge Edwin Bryant Crocker. The collec-tion now includes pottery from the fifth century B.C. through contemporary works of art. Tile and parquet floors, rococo mirrors, frescoed ceilings, handcrafted woodwork, and curving staircases make the building itself a work of art. Concerts, lectures, and other special events are scheduled throughout the year.

GOVERNOR'S MANSION

Sixteenth and H Streets, Sacramento. (916) 323-3047. Tours every half hour from 10 to 4:30 and by appointment daily. Adults, 50¢.

The official residence of California's thirteen governors from 1903 to

The Governor's Mansion

1967 is now a handsome Victorian museum that incorporates the history of the state. Living rooms, bedrooms, dining rooms, and hallways are furnished in a melange of styles to reflect their different inhabitants. The old carriage house has also been converted to a museum where you may see the hats, fans, parasols, and other personal belongings of the governors and their families.

FAIRYTALE TOWN

William Land Park, Sacramento. (916) 449-5233, Tuesday–Sunday, 10–5; closed December and January. Adults, $1; children, 50¢.

Nursery rhymes and favorite stories all seem quite plausible in this cheerful land of make-believe. Youngsters can crawl through the holes of The Cheese or down The Rabbit's Hole, pet the baby goats at Troll Bridge, see Hiawatha, the Three Little Pigs, the Tortoise, and Mary's Little Lamb. Cinderella's pumpkin coach, King Arthur's Castle, wonderful slides, and the Japanese garden, representing a Japanese children's story, complete the array. Just remember: "Please do not sit on the elves."

In the amusement center across the road, carousel and pony rides are available weekends, 11–5, weekdays in summer 11–4:30. Pony rides are 75¢ each, and the other nine rides are 50¢ each.

SACRAMENTO ZOO

3930 West Land Park Drive, Land Park, Sacramento. (916) 447-5094. Daily, 9–4. Adults, $2; ages 6–12, 50¢. (The zoo actually closes at 5 P.M. but the zookeeper thinks his zoo is special enough that it takes at least an hour to enjoy it—so he closes the gates at 4, disappointing all those who believe the posted times!)

Over 700 animals live in this tree-shaded garden and zoo. The reptile house is a favorite; others are the wallaroos, the flamingos, and the island of monkeys. The river otters have a slide for speedy entry into their pond and the penguins swim smugly in their pool. New orangutan, tiger, lion, and flamingo exhibits show these beautiful animals in a natural setting.

OLD SACRAMENTO

Sacramento was the major transportation hub for north-central California, providing a convenient location where water and land transportation systems could meet. Today, along the Sacramento River where Captain John Sutter established his Embarcadero in 1839, an important part of Sacramento's history is being restored to its former glory. Fifty-three structures built during the boom of the Gold Rush stand as living memorials to their past, looking as they did in the 1850s and 1860s. Inside are restaurants, stores, offices, and museums. For tour information, call (916) 445-4209.

The Old Eagle Theater at Front and J Streets, opened on October 18, 1849, now presents old melodramas and contemporary plays. (Box office information: 446-6761. Tours daily, between 10 and 4. Free.)

Central Pacific Passenger Station at Front and J (322-3676; 10–5 daily, free with Railroad Museum ticket) is a reconstruction of a station that existed here in 1876. Waiting rooms, ticket offices, baggage rooms, and railroad cars tell their stories through tour wands.

Old Sacramento Schoolhouse at Front and L (383-2636), looks just as it did in the 1880s and is open 9:30–4:30, Monday–Saturday; 12–4:30 on Sunday; free.

B.F. Hastings Museum at Second and J (445-4655, 10–5 daily; free) was the first western terminus of the Pony Express and the Sacramento office of Wells Fargo. Wells Fargo and Pony Express exhibits fascinate, as do the reconstructed Supreme Court rooms and posters on the early post office system.

Huntington-Hopkins Hardware Store (1131 I Street, 323-7234; 10–5 daily; free) is a reconstruction of one of the West's most historic hardware stores and includes a small museum of hardware.

The bookstores, ice cream and candy stores, fun house of game machines, boutiques, and restaurants make Old Sacramento a full day's adventure. Lady Adams, which houses a cookie and music box store, is the oldest existing building in Old Sacramento, made from materials shipped round the Horn in 1852.

CALIFORNIA STATE RAILROAD MUSEUM

Second and I Streets, Old Sacramento. (916) 445-7373. Reservations: 445-4209. Daily, 10–5. Adults, $3; ages 6–17, $1.

This state-of-the-art new museum combines slide shows, theater presentations, panel exhibits, dioramas, and railroad cars to walk in and around to show how trains have affected our history and culture. Lucius Beebe's elegant private car; the Railway Post Office Car, where you can try your hand at sorting mail; and the rocking St. Hyacinthe Sleeper are some of the special attractions. The museum also has steam train excursions and presentations.

SACRAMENTO SCIENCE CENTER AND JUNIOR MUSEUM

3615 Auburn Boulevard, east area, Sacramento. (916) 485-4471. Monday–Friday, 9:30–4; Sunday, 12–5. Adults, $2; children, $1.

Live animals indigenous to California live in the museum, which also offers special films and exhibits, and supervised playtime with the animals on weekends.

SILVER WINGS AVIATION MUSEUM

Mather Air Force Base, Building 3860, Rancho Cordova. (916) 364-2177. 10–4, weekdays; 12–4, weekends. Free.

Military and civilian aircraft displays and fifty-five films dating from the Wright Brothers to Vietnam (shown continuously, by request) are presented in this reproduction of a 1914 hangar. There are World War I and World War II aviation displays, displays on pioneer women, engines, and models. The Teeny-Genie, an experimental pleasure plane with a VW engine, is wonderful. Travis Air Force Base plans a museum which will house a Douglas A-26 Invader, an F-102, and other aircraft.

The Mather Planetarium in Rancho Cordova, (916) 364-2908, is open to groups of twelve or more by reservation. You'll see stars, planets, comets, meteor showers, outlines of constellations, and other space phenomena on a domed ceiling.

Aviators who'd rather do than see can contact the River City Balloon Company, 3444 Vougue Court, Sacramento, CA 95826, (916) 362-2000, for balloon flights.

The Teeny-Genie

NIMBUS FISH HATCHERY

2001 Nimbus Road, Rancho Cordova. (916) 355-0666. Daily, 8–4. Free.

After fighting their way from the Pacific Ocean, salmon and steelhead spawn here each fall and winter. The hatchery has a capacity of twenty million salmon eggs and accounts for 60 to 70 percent of the commercial catch off the California Coast.

GIBSON RANCH COUNTY PARK

8552 Gibson Ranch Road, Elverta (take Watt Avenue north to Elverta Road). (916) 366-2061. Daily 7 A.M. to dusk. Free.

This 326-acre park is really a working farm. There are cows, hens, and horses to feed. Muskrats, ducks, and geese swim in the lake, which you can fish. There are ponies and donkeys to ride, paddleboats to rent, old buggies and a blacksmith shop to see, and picnics and hayrides to enjoy. Tours by appointment.

FOLSOM PROJECT DAM AND POWERPLANT

7806 Folsom-Auburn Road, Folsom. (916) 988-1707. Tours: Tuesday–Saturday, 10 A.M. and 1 P.M. Free.

Drive on top of the dam and past the gorgeous lake to get to the powerhouse. Tours pass three generators—with capacities of 66,240 kilowatts each—and go through the dam, depending upon how many people are visiting at the time.

FOLSOM CITY PARK AND ZOO

50 Natoma Street, Folsom. (916) 355-7200. Daily, 10–4, except Monday. Free.

This unique small zoo specializes in California native animals, with some exciting exotic imports. Many of the animals were raised as pets, some are handicapped, none can live wild. The free roaming flock of more than 50 peafowl delights visitors. A one-third scale live steam train runs weekends in summer and fall (50¢).

Historic Sutter Street, in Folsom, is a restored section of old buildings and shops. The miniatures at Dorothea's Peppermint Lane and Patsy's Soda Parlor take visitors back to gayer times; and the Sutter Gaslight Theater, a cider shop, and many ethnic restaurants make a short stay worthwhile. At Sutter and Wool Streets, the reconstructed Southern Pacific depot displays historical treasures.

The Folsom Powerhouse, on Riley Street, relayed electricity to Sacramento from 1895 to 1952. For tours call (916) 988-0205.

CALIFORNIA RAILWAY MUSEUM

10 miles east of Fairfield on Highway 12, Rio Vista Junction. (707) 374-2978. Weekends and holidays, 12–5. Daily in summer. Free entrance to the park and museum. Rides: adults, $1.50; children, 75¢, all day.

The California Railway Museum was put together by a nonprofit organization of men who love trains. You can walk through and around the more than sixty retired trolleys and steam locomotives or just watch the railroad buffs at work. An old-fashioned Salt Lake & Utah observation car is there for the dreaming (remember Judy Garland and "The Harvey Girls?"), as are Birney Street "dinkeys," an electric cable car, a New York City "El," a Pullman car that's been made up, a Gay Nineties San Francisco street car, a Toonerville Trolley from the Key System, and lots more. The gift shop at the entrance holds the largest collection of railroad books in the West, along with cards, model kits, old ads, tickets, and badges. Picnic areas are available, and rides are frequent on weekends.

RIO VISTA MUSEUM

16 North Front Street, Rio Vista. (707) 374-5169. Weekends, 2–5 and by appointment. Free.

All of the treasures in this little museum have been donated by local residents. There are antique etchings and photos; newspapers and books; and farm implements such as tools, plows, a buggy, a wagon, a forge and a foundry, typewriters, a wine press, Chinese hats, and local birds' eggs. The museum was created during the Bicentennial, "So," says its curator, "we won't forget all about the past."

MICKE GROVE PARK AND ZOO AND SAN JOAQUIN COUNTY HISTORICAL MUSEUM

11793 North Micke Grove Road, 3 miles south of Lodi on Highway 99/5. Park phone: (209) 944-2444. Museum: 963-4119. Park hours: dawn to dusk daily. $2.50 per car on weekends and holidays. Zoo: 10–5 daily. Free. Museum: 10–5 Wednesday–Sunday. Free.

"Man and Nature Hand in Hand" is the theme of this remarkable multi-building museum created for the Bicentennial. A trotter's sulky greets you at the door of the main building, which focuses on the home. A millinery shop, Victorian sitting room, and dining room are meticulously furnished. The exhibits are changed continuously. We saw a beautiful collection of quilts and "Needle/Shuttle and Awl," an interpretation of the techniques employed by Native American women in the manufacture and decoration of items of utilitarian and ceremonial use.

A completely outfitted Liberty Harness shop is on the grounds as are a ranch blacksmith shop and a schoolhouse that seems to be just waiting for children. One barn concentrates on the grapes, fruits, and nuts produced in the area; another focuses on the River Delta, the Indians of the marshland, and the conquering of water and soil. "Earth is here so kind, that just tickle her with a hoe and she laughs up a harvest," is what one Delta farmer wrote. A large building filled with plows, hoes, wagons, forks, axes, and farm implements of every other kind shows how the harvesting was—and is still—done.

Lions, bobcats, green monkeys, grey foxes, kinkajous, pumas, and black leopards are some of the animals in the nice little zoo. There are public feedings of the birds and animals at one o'clock every day.

Picnic areas, an amusement park with lots of kiddie rides, a swimming pool, and peaceful rose and Japanese gardens add to the attraction of this pleasant park.

POLLARDVILLE GHOST TOWN

10464 Highway 99/5, 3 miles above Stockton. (209) 931-0272/4571. Weekends, 12–6. Closed in rainy season. Adults, 50¢; children and seniors, 25¢.

Pollardville Ghost Town is made up of both movie set and real buildings brought down from the Mother Lode country. The Jamestown Jail was brought from Calaveras County and the Freedom Gazette newspaper building from Jackson. The hotel starred in Gregory Peck's "Big Country." Gunfights are staged and you can ride the Rock & Roll Railroad as it barrels around town on its regular runs (50¢). Visitors can see an 1880s livery stable, a dentist's and doctor's office, and an undertaker's establishment. Vaudeville and melodrama are present at the old Palace Theater on weekends in the summer. The Chicken Kitchen, at the entrance, dispenses chicken dinners in an Old West atmosphere.

THE HAGGIN MUSEUM

1201 North Pershing Avenue, Victory Park, Stockton. (209) 462-4116. Daily 1:30–5, except Mondays and holidays. Free.

Three floors of history and art fill this handsome brick building. Interpretive displays of California and local history include an arcade of nineteenth century storefronts, arms and mining lamps, vehicle galleries, and an Indian Room. See memorabilia of Stockton's past, and a gorgeous green and red harvesting machine. The art galleries include works by California artists such as Albert Bierstadt. Our kids honed in on the letter by Daniel Boone, the Donner party relics, the port diorama, and the display of one hundred years of dolls.

PIXIE WOODS

Louis Park, Stockton. (209) 466-9890/944-8220. Fall and spring weekends, 12–6; Wednesday–Friday, 11–5; weekends 12–7 in summer. Closed from Halloween to Easter Week. Over 12, 50¢; under, 30¢. Train and boat rides: 30¢; Merry-go-round 30¢.

When you enter the rainbow gate of Pixie Woods, you enter a children's fairyland built entirely by the people of Stockton. Children can play in a castle, on a pirate ship, around a rocket ship, and on a fire engine. They can ride on a Chinese dragon and slide down a colored slide, and talk to Little Miss Muffet. The volcano erupts regularly in Pirate's Cove. At MacGregor's Farm, you can pet pigs, sheep, rabbits, and Billy Goats Gruff. You can even have parties with Alice in Wonderland.

MILLER HORSE AND BUGGY RANCH

9425 Yosemite Boulevard at Highway 132, Modesto. (209) 522-1781. Open "whenever Mrs. Mae Miller is there, which is most of the time." Reservations preferred. Adults, $2; children under 12, 50¢.

This wagon collection and 1900 general store are absolutely fascinating, but they are so cluttered that some people may shy away. Those who climb in and poke around will be well rewarded. Over fifty cars and wagons, including stagecoaches, fire engines, beer wagons, racing sulkies, Victoria coaches, excursion buses, and an ambulance used in the San Francisco earthquake are in the barn. A hurdy-gurdy and high-button shoes, sausage stuffers, old typewriters, and a bicycle collection dating to the 1820s (including a mother-of-pearl tandem bike reputedly given to Lillian Russell by "Diamond Jim" Brady) are in the store.

Folsom Park

In Modesto proper a new Victorian museum, the McHenry Mansion (1402 I Street, 577-5366, 12–4 except Monday, free) is being put together. You'll see gold mining artifacts, World War I relics, old fashioned rooms, and more.

PUBLIC RELATIONS TOURS

CALIFORNIA ALMOND GROWERS EXCHANGE. *Seventeenth and C Streets, Sacramento. (916) 446-8409. Monday–Friday, 9, 10, 1, and 2. Saturday movie only at 11 and 3. Free. Groups by appointment.* Franciscan fathers brought the almond from Spain to California in 1769. Today, Blue Diamond is the world's largest almond packer. Visitors see many unusual machines designed to sort, crack, halve, slice, dice, and roast almonds. You see concrete bins eight stories high, a mile-long conveyor belt, and an explanatory movie on the hour-long tour. Then dig into the twelve different flavored almonds in the tasting room (open 8–5:30 weekdays, 10–4 Saturday).

HERSHEY CHOCOLATE COMPANY. *1400 South Yosemite Avenue, Oakdale. (209) 847-0381. Monday–Friday, 8:15–3, by appointment. Free.* Candy bars, chocolate kisses, and chocolate syrups are made, weighed, packaged, and labeled in the course of this thirty-minute tour. You pass huge chocolate vats, candy-bar molds in action, and rooms for the processing of instant cocoa and chocolate syrup.

THE GOLD COUNTRY

To drive along Highway 49 is to experience California's colorful history and legends. This is the Gold Country—the land of writers like Mark Twain, Bret Harte, and Joaquin Miller, bandits like Black Bart and Joaquin Murietta, and heroes like Ulysses S. Grant and Horatio Alger. Passing through little towns named Copperopolis and Jenny Lind, visitors who look carefully will see the traces of the hundreds of thousands of people—Cornish, Welsh, English, German, French, Italian, Mexican, Peruvian, Australian, Chinese, and African—who migrated to this place seeking fame and fortune. The town of Volcano still has an old Chinese store and a Jewish cemetery. The many parks and campgrounds are inevitably near quiet streams that once teemed with gold panners. In Gold Country you'll find the only town in the United States ever to name itself a nation: Rough and Ready seceded from the Union on April 7, 1850, to become a republic with its own president, constitution, and flag. (By July fourth, it had slipped quietly back into the United States.) The best thing to do in the Gold Country is just explore and talk to the natives; you'll have good experiences that you couldn't possibly find listed in a book and you'll hear about towns that exist now only in memory.

RAIL TOWN 1897 AND THE SIERRA RAILWAY COMPANY

Off Highways 49 and 108 on Fifth Avenue, Jamestown. (209) 984-3953. Daily in summer, 10–5; and weekends, fall and spring. Roundhouse tours: over 16, $1.95; 5–15, 95¢. Varying prices for special train rides, twilight cruises, and weekend excursions by rail, starting at $8.95 for adults, $4.50 for ages 5–15 (including roundhouse tour).

The Sierra's Mother Lode Cannonball steam engine speeds for an hour through the Mother Lode near the town of Chinese Camp. At the Jamestown station, you'll see a working blacksmith shop, wood shop, car repair shops, a machine shop still powered by belts, the turntable, and the roundhouse. The locomotives here appear in movies frequently, so you may recognize them. We saw an old green engine loaded with wood ready for its role in a Jesse James movie. For tickets and information: Sierra Railway, P.O. Box 1250, Jamestown, CA 95327.

The town of Jamestown has been completely restored and there are many interesting stores and restaurants there and in the Victorian park in the center of town.

TUOLUMNE COUNTY MUSEUM AND HISTORY CENTER

158 West Bradford, Sonora. (209) 532-1317. 9–4:30 Monday–Friday, 10–3:30 weekends in summer. Free.

Located in an 1857 jail, this thriving museum offers Mark Twain in vignette, surrounded by Twain memorabilia, an 1890s Victorian vignette, and an old-fashioned men's store window display. The six geographical regions of Tuolumne County are depicted in photos and artifacts. In the east cellblock, you'll find an old gunshop in one cell, a cowboy bunkhouse in another. We're particularly taken with the foot warmer used by stagecoach drivers. Youngsters will enjoy Bill West's paintings of cowboys and horses.

SONORA

The town of Sonora, once called "The Queen of the Southern Mines" is a great place to browse. Stop in at the *Sonora Fire Department Museum* in City Hall (94 North Washington Street, 532-4541, daily, free) to see uniforms, Currier & Ives prints of fires, silver speaking trumpets, and a fire alert system. The *Archeology and History* display in the Francisco Building (48 West Yaney Street, daily, free) shows bottles, fragments, and objects found on the site of the building during construction. Another display case contains memorabilia from the 1854 Union Democrat, including old type, photos, bill heads, and old editions.

COLUMBIA STATE HISTORIC PARK

Highway 49, Columbia. (209) 532-4301. Daily 9–5, except holidays. Free.

Columbia, "The Gem of the Southern Mines," is a restored goldmining town of the 1850s. The streets and wooden sidewalks lead you to buildings, stores, and eateries outfitted as they were in the town's heyday. The Columbia Gazette office, open to the public on weekends and all summer, still prints a small newspaper; the Columbia Candy Kitchen still sells hand-dipped penny candy; the 1857 Douglas Saloon still dispenses an occasional draft along with the sarsaparilla. Peek into the carpenter's shop; the ice depot; and the schoolhouse, which is furnished with bell tower, pump organ, desks and potbellied stoves. The Chinese herb shop, the fandango hall, and the town jail and drugstore are all Main Street attractions. Fallon House, which once starred Lola Montez and Edwin Booth, has a summer repertory company. The gold scales in the Wells Fargo office weighed out over $55 million in dust and nuggets of the $87 million mined here. At the Hidden Treasure Gold Mine Tour (532-9693, $5 for adults, $2.50 for children) you can try your hand at panning. The park museum offers exhibits on the Indians, the Chinese population (once one-sixth of Columbia), and, of course, the gold miners. The collection of old dolls and toys is noteworthy. Picnic spots are available, so plan to spend an enjoyable day in this thriving town of yesteryear.

MOANING CAVE

Vallecito, on the road between Columbia State Historic Park and Highway 4. (209) 736-2708. Open 9–6 daily in summer and on weekends in winter, 10–5 winter weekdays; closed Christmas. Adults $3.95; ages 6–11, $1.95.

You can count the 144 winding steps that lead you 165 feet down to a graveyard of prehistoric bones and moaning winds. You'll see fantastic rock formations, such as Elephant's Ears and the Little Girl's Face, that add to the eerie feeling that you're intruding on unknown spirits. The main chamber is large enough to hold the Statue of Liberty. Picnic tables and a view of the hills offer a pleasant waiting space, as does the exhibit-filled waiting room. Stalactites hang "tight" from the ceiling and stalagmites are "mighty mounds" on the floor—that's how we remember which is which. Moaning Cave also offers a three-hour Adventure Tour for $25.

Nearby, the California Caverns at Cave City (Mountain Ranch Road,

The Sierra Railroad

north of Murphys; 10–5 in summer, 10–4 in fall, daily; closed rainy season; (209) 736-2708; adults $4, 6–12 $2) offers a "Trail of Lights" tour once taken by John Muir amid lakes and crystalline jungles. For information on their three- and five-hour "Wild Cave" tours, write Box 78, Vallecito, CA 95251.

OLD TIMERS MUSEUM

Main Street, Murphys. Winter weekends 10–5 and Wednesday–Sunday, in summer. 25¢.

An old time bedroom, bar, furnished blacksmith shop, portrait of J. Pierpont Morgan, and an antique bicycle are the highpoints of this old-fashioned assemblage of gold-mining memories.

Down the block, The Peppermint Stick (728-3570) entices with old-fashioned sodas and sundaes, creations such as "Claim Jumpers" and the "Pick and Shovel Special," and peppermint ice cream cones for travelers on the run.

MERCER CAVERNS

Ebbetts Pass Highway, 1 mile from Murphys. (209) 728-2101. Daily 9–5 in summer; 11–4 winter weekends and holidays. Adults, $3.50; ages 5–11, $1.75.

This thirty-minute tour past stalactites and stalagmites, aragonites, and helictites takes you into a subterranean wonderland. Eerie rock formations like the Organ Loft, Angel Wings, and the Chinese Meat Market are dazzling examples of the artistry of nature. Mercer Caverns was discovered in 1885 by a tired, thirsty prospector, Walter J. Mercer, who noticed bay bushes growing near a limestone bluff and thought he had found water.

ANGELS CAMP MUSEUM

753 Main Street, Angels Camp, on Highway 49. (209) 736-2963. 10–4 daily in summer, on weekends in winter and Tuesday and Wednesday in winter. Adults, 50¢; ages 6–12, 25¢.

A mortician's embalming kit and hearse, models of a stamp mill and the Wild Goose Mine, a cheese press and a waffle iron, minerals, gemstones, and hunks of quartz containing gold are the main attractions in this cluttered museum. A rusty old fire engine, petrified wood, cave stalactites, and exotic old mining machines surround the building.

If you stay on Highway 49 between Columbia and Angels Camp, you may want to stop for a peek into a replica of Mark Twain's Cabin on Jackass Hill. Here he gathered material for his *Jumping Frog of Calaveras County* and wrote *Roughing It*—this was a turning point in his career.

CALAVERAS COUNTY HISTORICAL MUSEUM

Main Street, San Andreas. (209) 754-4203. Daily, 10–4. Courthouse tours by appointment. Adults, 50¢; children, 25¢.

The Calaveras County Courthouse and County Jail of 1867 has been transformed into a beautifully designed treasure house. You can walk through the judge's chambers (where the judge's robe still hangs) and then go downstairs to see the cell where Black Bart awaited trial. The Comanche Catholic Church is inside a huge safe. There's a large exhibit of Miwok Indian artifacts. The representative bedroom and parlor, miner's cabin, and general store are extremely well-done and well-labeled. Much of the work on the County Courthouse was done as a Bicentennial project.

Down the stairs to Mercer Caverns fantasy world.

AMADOR COUNTY MUSEUM

225 Church Street, Jackson. (209) 223-3230 ext. 386. Wednesday–Sunday, 10–4. Donation.

Working models—built to a scale of one inch to the foot and using original materials—of the North Star Mine stamp, the Kennedy Mine Tailing Wheel No. 2,and the Kennedy Mine head frame are demonstrated by appointment. The museum collection also includes other mining artifacts, musical and medical instruments, an oak chest used to carry water on an 1852 covered wagon, and a folding chair and foot-operated drill used by a traveling dentist.

One mile out North Main Street, there are two wheels on each side of the road, fifty-eight feet in diameter. They were used to transport waste from the mine. The Kennedy Tailing Wheels are almost lost in history, but their size is still impressive.

INDIAN GRINDING ROCK STATE HISTORIC PARK

Pine Grove–Volcano Road, Volcano. (209) 296-7448. Daily, weather permitting. Day use per car: $2.

When you walk up to the top of the hill, all you see is a huge, flat rock with a few pockmarks and scratchy lines, surrounded by a wooden fence. Then you get closer and see that the scratchy lines are petroglyphs by the Miwok Indians to commemorate their tales of hunting and fishing. The pockmarks are actually mortar holes—1,185 of them—in which the Indian women ground the seeds, bulbs, fungi, and acorns that served as the staples of their diet. Each of the mortar holes was abandoned when it became too deep. The acorn meal was sifted and washed many times to remove bitterness, then the meal was mixed with water in a basket, and heated by hot rocks dropped into the mush. One family consumed two thousand pounds of acorn a year. An extensive Indian Cultural Center and Museum, incorporating Miwok bark houses, a ceremonial roundhouse, and a corn granary is now being built. The center offers interpretive information, classes in Indian crafts, and Miwok Indians participating in the sharing of the Indian spirit.

In Volcano itself, The Jug and Rose Confectionary Shop has been serving breakfasts, lunches, and sweets garnished with fresh flowers since 1855. Prices are modest and children are made especially welcome at their own small table.

CHEW KEE STORE

Fiddletown, just off Highway 49 outside Plymouth.

Built in the 1850s, the Chew Kee Store is believed to be California's only surviving rammed-earth structure of the Gold Rush era and has been called "a truly remarkable showcase for history frozen in time." A small shrine, a lantern made from a five-gallon oil can, ceramic rice crocks, pipes, brass opium cans, food safes, gambling hall receipts, a long black queue in a glass display case, and the full stock of a Chinese herb store will soon be on view as the store becomes part of the state parks system.

SAM'S TOWN AMERICANA MUSEUM

Cameron Park, Highway 80, Shingle Springs. (916) 933-1662/677-2273. Sunday—Thursday, 8—7:30; Friday and Saturday, 8—9:30. $1 adults, under 7 and over 70, free.

Sam's is a town, restaurant, and amusement park all in one. The front of the building looks like an old town, with doctor's office, stable, saloon, and theater; inside it is one large building divided into restaurants, a gift and book shop, a honky-tonk piano bar, a fun arcade, and the Americana Museum. Thirty scenes portray fine old times from the days of the steam horse-drawn fire engine, to Jenny Lind and Lillian Russell in concert, to old Saturday Night Bath Time. Vintage vehicles—paddy wagons, trolley cars, buggies, surreys and chariots—stand on the grounds.

EL DORADO COUNTY HISTORICAL MUSEUM

El Dorado County Fairgrounds, Placerville. (916) 626-2250. Wednesday—Saturday, 10—4; Sunday, 12—3:30. Free.

Gold mining and history of the farming pioneers are focal points for this relatively new collection. A seed broadcaster mounted on a Spring wagon and pulled by horses; a mammoth universal concentrator, or shaking table, on flexible legs (it could separate the gold from one-and a half tons of mercury hardrock ore per hour); and a walk-in Shay engine No. 4, once used to pull logs and equipment, grabbed the kids' attention here.

GOLD BUG MINE

Bedford Park, Placerville. (916) 622-0832. Daily. Free.

The only municipally owned, open-to-the-public gold mine in the world was worked as recently as 1947. The longer shaft of the mine ends at an exposed gold-bearing quartz vein. The occasional drip of water rings in the cool, eerie silence of the tunnel. The huge gold-stamp mill by the creek is still undergoing restoration.

Placerville itself was called Old Hangtown, after the Hanging Tree in the center of town. A walk through the town, from the Ponly Express Harness Shop at 3030 Sacramento, which used to be the Western Terminus of the Pony Express in 1861, to the Wells Fargo Office, once the scene of busy gold shipments, will illustrate its history.

East on Highway 50, the Camino Narrow Gauge Railway runs on weekends from 11 to 5. The Michigan-California Lumber Company nearby arranges tours which begin with uncut logs and end with lumber being loaded into freight cars.

GHOST MOUNTAIN

Pollack Pines, Highway 50 above Placerville. (916) 644-2415. Daily in summer, weekends in winter, weather permitting.

Day visitors to this campground can stroll through a Wells Fargo Office, the jail, the general store, the Indian village and museum, an old-time hotel and chapel; ride a pony or stagecoach; and join in a Western barbecue. A complete ghost town is being rebuilt in which every building will house a working craftsman to show you what life was like in Gold Rush days.

MARSHALL GOLD DISCOVERY STATE HISTORIC PARK

Highway 49, Coloma. (916) 622-3470. Daily 10–5 except holidays. Adult state parks ticket, 50¢. Picnicking $2 per car.

Sutter's Mill has risen again on the American River. The museum is modern—a complete exhibit of the discovery of gold and the lives of the gold miners. There are maps, tools, and mementos of the miners; a pictorial display of the discovery; an exhibit of the Gold Rush routes; and a piece of timber from the first mill. Gold dust and nuggets, geological exhibits, and the story of the Maidu Indians are also displayed, along with the diary of miner F. C. Negler and dioramas of history. There are Gold Rush films and programs three times a day in summer and winter weekends. On the grounds you'll find self-guided displays, concessions with various interpretative themes from 1847 to 1900, an 1860 general store and bank, and a Chinese store. The table in the Mormon workers' cabin is set for dinner. The miner's cabin is furnished with a tin of coffee, cans of beans, a scale, a Bible, and the miner himself, in bed with his boots on. The blacksmith shop, gunsmith shop, arrastre (ore crusher), and hydraulic mining displays are also of interest. But the best thing of all is to stand next to the big wheel of the mill and look at this quiet spot that changed history. The ranger has been known to saw a log or two in the mill on weekends.

PLACER COUNTY HISTORICAL MUSEUM

Gold Country Fairgrounds, 1273 High Street, Auburn. (916) 885-9570. Daily, 8–4. Adults, $1; ages 6–16 and over 65, 50¢.

Old mining equipment and pioneer mementos depict the early days of Placer County. The colorful calliope and stained-glass model of the county courthouse and the wishing well are special favorites. Birds nests, blackjacks, an olive press, and the wooden washing machine in the replica kitchen also drew comment. Local school children can participate in the Living History programs that include gold-panning lessons and tasting Indian acorn soup.

In nearby Old Town, antique shops and an old-fashioned tower firehouse are open for inspection.

NORTH STAR MINE POWERHOUSE MUSEUM

Lower Mill Street, at Empire, Grass Valley. (916) 273-9853. Daily 11–5 in summer; 11–4 Saturday and Sunday in winter. Adult ticket, 50¢.

Built by A. D. Foote in 1875, this is the first completely water-powered compressed-air transmission plant of its kind. The compressed air, generated by ten-ton, thirty-foot Pelton waterwheels, furnished power for the entire mine. The museum houses photos, ore specimens, enticing safes, mining dioramas, models of mines, an assaying laboratory, carbide lamps, and "widowmaker" drill bits, but the main attractions are the wheels, suspension bridges, and walkways of the building itself.

Down the block, the Grass Valley Museum in Mount St. Mary's (on South Church; 12–3 Wednesday, Saturday and Sunday in summer; 273-9874; 50¢) offers vintage furnishings including an 1880s doctor's office, a school room, children's bedrooms, and convent artifacts such as the silver press used for making the Host.

Further along on Mill Street are the homes of Lola Montez and Lotta Crabtree. Lola was a Bavarian singer, dancer, and king's favorite who fled to America in 1853 when her king fell from power. Lotta Crabtree was Lola's protégée and soon became famous, rich, and beloved by the American public. Lola's home is open to the public daily (12–4, free) in the summer.

EMPIRE MINE STATE HISTORIC PARK

10791 East Empire Street, Central Park, Grass Valley. (916) 273-8522. Daily 9–5, except holidays; tours by appointment. Adult parks ticket, 50¢.

Telling the story of hard-rock gold mining and its significance in California's history, the Empire is the oldest, largest, and richest gold mine in the area. Many of the sixteen stopping points along the mine's self-guiding tour are in ruins or the events exist only in memory and the sites are being reconstructed. Movies are shown to help excite your imagination. "Gone too are the hundreds of Cornish miners who dug the 367 miles of tunnels to a depth of nearly 12,000 feet on the incline, over a mile below the surface; gone are the hoists that lowered the men the thousands of feet down the shaft; gone are the mules that pulled the ore trains through the tunnels. But the gold is still there, awaiting a time when mining it will again be profitable."

NEVADA COUNTY HISTORICAL SOCIETY MUSEUMS

Firehouse No. 1, Main and Commercial Streets, Nevada City. (916) 265-9941. Daily 11–4 in summer, closed winter Mondays. Donation.

The most frequently photographed item in the firehouse is a photographic portrait of an early mine owner whose own image as a twelve-year-old boy mysteriously appeared at his left shoulder when the photographer developed the negative more than ninety years ago. Other spirits supposedly rearrange the exhibits at night and prod visitors by day. A glowing Chinese altar, Maidu artifacts, relics of the Donner party, children's toys and books, and pioneer mementos fill this museum to overflowing. The new transportation exhibit includes snowshoes for horses and memories of the "Never

Come Never Go Railroad." On display in Pioneer Park are vehicles representing transportation in the old days—a beer wagon, stagecoach, logging truck, and firehouse carts and wagons. There's also a small history museum in the Searls Library (1–4 except Sunday, off Main Street).

The American Victorian Museum (325 Spring Street; 265-5804; 9:30–4 except Tuesday and during dinner; free) occupies the 1856 Miners Foundry, which manufactured the famous Pelton waterwheel. The museum collects, preserves, and exhibits artifacts of the Victorian Era including an 1887 Dutch Street organ, an 1871 pipe organ, and a 1913 theater organ, plus graphics, paintings, games, and toys. Meals are served in the uniquely decorated Foundry room and repertory theater is offered on weekends. Museum personnel can also show you the 1873 *Martin Luther Marsh House,* a Victorian Italianate residence at 254 Boulder Street, by appointment.

MALAKOFF DIGGINS STATE HISTORIC PARK

North Bloomfield. 17 miles northeast of Nevada City on a crooked mountain road. (916) 265-2740. Daily 10–5 in summer; weekends in fall and spring, 12–4. 50¢.

Many millions of dollars' worth of gold poured from these huge hydraulic diggings, and a small sign informs visitors that there's still enough gold left here, and on other sites throughout the Gold Country, to mine $12 million worth annually for the next fifty years. The museum displays a model of the monitor used in the gold mines, showing how hydraulic mining worked. Photos of the two-mile Bloomfield tunnel, the twelve-foot-long skis used by miners, a portable undertaker's table, mementos of the Chinese miners, and an old-time bar and poker room are some of the highlights. Other buildings and the gold mine itself can be seen on walking tours.

SIERRA COUNTY MUSEUM

Main Street, Downieville. Daily 9:30–4 in summer and by appointment. Free.

Keepsakes of the hardy pioneers of Downieville are housed in this old stone building. Outside is a scale model of an arrastre from the Sierra Buttes Mine that crushed ore more finely than the tailings from a stamp mill, along with a hand-operated 100-year-old valve used to control water pressure in the early hydraulic diggings at Morristown.

KENTUCKY MINE MUSEUM

Highway 49, Sierra City. (916) 862-1310. Wednesday–Sunday, 10–5; daily mid-June to mid-September; weekends when weather permits, and by appointment. Tour: Adults, $1.50; under 12 free. Museum: 50¢ for adults.

A five-stamp mill built in the 1870s, a 1928 ten-stamp mill, and a hard-rock gold mine are shown during a fascinating forty-minute tour. The tour explains the process of hard-rock mining from beginning to end—from mining to milling. The stamp mill is one of the only mills in the area which is still operable, with all original machinery intact. The Pelton waterwheels which provided power to run the mining machinery are also intact. The museum shows constantly changing displays from Sierra County's past, including mining equipment, logging machinery, clothing, old skis, household articles, and a schoolroom exhibit.

PLUMAS-EUREKA STATE PARK MUSEUM

Off Highway 89, Johnsville. (916) 836-2380. Daily 8–5 in summer; until 4:30 spring and fall; closed holidays. Free.

Snowshoe Thompson used to carry sixty to eighty pounds of mail on his back over the Sierra in winter for the miners. A pair of his skis are presented in this fully packed museum, along with hard-rock mining displays, an assay office, models of a stamp mill and an arrastre, natural history exhibits, and pioneer life exhibits.

LA PORTE MUSEUM

Main Street, Quincy. (916) 675-2905.

The Clamper's Historical Society, *E. Clampus Vitus,* which cares for widows and orphans of miners, is presently constructing a museum of mining artifacts which will be open to the public. An old mining steam engine, fishing tackle, and tall stories are now being collected in this northernmost mining town of the Mother Lode.

DONNER MEMORIAL STATE PARK

Donner Lake, Truckee. (916) 587-3841. Daily 10–12 and 1–4 winter weekends, weather permitting. Adults, 50¢; ages 6–17, 25¢.

The Emigrant Trail museum combines natural history with one of the most dramatic of human stories. Man's conquest of the Sierra Nevada and the tragic story of the Donner party are told with relics, dioramas, pictures, and models. During the disastrous winter of 1846, a party of 189 tried to make it to California. Only forty-seven people survived. The pedestal of the memorial to the Donner Party is twenty-two feet high, symbolic of the twenty-two foot early snowfall that trapped them. Chinese railroad workers, the "Big Four" railroad tycoons, miners, and mountain men are also remembered here.

LAKE TAHOE

Visitors Center, Highway 89, South Lake Tahoe. (916) 544-5050. Road conditions: (800) 822-5977.

Lake Tahoe is world-famous for its crystal-clear water and beautiful surroundings. Visitors can ski, water-ski, boat, swim (but only in August unless you're a polar bear), sun, backpack and hike, or just enjoy the forest wilderness. Naturalist programs are given on summer weekends in the D. L. Bliss and Emerald Bay State Parks and at Camp Richardson. Movies and shows are held in the Lake of the Sky Amphitheater. Tahoe Cruises, boats and sea-plane rides are also available (525-7143/546-3185). If you can, take a cruise on the *M.S. Dixie Paddlewheeler* (702) 588-3508. The boat is berthed at Zephyr Cove, eight miles north of Stateline.

The *Boreal Alpine Slide* is a new Lake Tahoe adventure that combines bobsledding and tray-sliding and is open from 10 to 10 daily in summer, weekends in winter. A chairlift lifts you to the top of Boreal Mountain (ten

Heavenly Valley—South Lake Tahoe

miles west of Truckee on Highway 80) and you swoosh down three thousand feet of straightaways, curves, and banked turns.

Vikingsholm, a thirty-eight-room Nordic fortress, is open to the public from 10 to 5 daily, in summer, on Emerald Bay's southwest shore.

The Lake Tahoe Historical Society Log Cabin Museum on Star Lake Avenue behind the fire station (10–4 daily in summer) features artifacts from Lake Tahoe's earliest days. The Gatekeeper's Log House (located at the outlet for the lake which is the headwaters of the Truckee River), is being restored on Highway 89 in Tahoe City as a museum. And the Ehrmann Mansion and the preserved cabin of General Phipps, one of Tahoe's first settlers, are being opened to the public in Sugarpine Point State Park.

The *Taylor Creek Stream Profile Chamber* near Camp Richardson is part of the El Dorado National Forest Visitors Center. You can take one of their self-guided nature walks through a mountain meadow and marsh and down into the chamber, where you look through glass windows to see the rainbow trout and aquatic life of a naturally flowing mountain stream. Recorded messages help you identify the fish and plants in front of you.

You may want to venture to the Nevada side of the lake for a visit to the *Ponderosa Ranch* (Incline Village; 702/831-0691; 10–5 daily in summer and weekends in early fall and late spring, $4.50 adults, $3.50, 6–16) to see the Cartwright Ranch House, Hoss's Mystery Mine, Frontier Town, an antique car and carriage museum, the Ponderosa barnyard, and other rides and attractions on this television-film set.

But you'll always head back to that glorious lake, named in the language of the Washoe Tribe "Big Water," gouged from the crown of the Sierra during the Ice Age.

THE FRESNO AREA

Some people think that Fresno exists only as a stopping off place from San Francisco to Los Angeles, but it's actually a big, booming city in its own right, with lots of good Armenian restaurants and a beautiful city park. The trip to Fresno is a good, long four hours by car from San Francisco, but there are so many motels in the city you can usually be assured of a room when you arrive. Surrounded by rich farmland, pretty lakes, and an impressive irrigation system, Fresno is also the entrance to Sierra National Forest and Sequoia, Kings Canyon, and Yosemite National Parks.

R. C. BAKER MEMORIAL MUSEUM

297 West Elm, Coalinga. (209) 935-1914. Monday–Friday, 9–12, 1 5; Saturday, 11–5; Sunday, 1–5. Free.
The newly remodeled R. C. Baker Museum, named in honor of a Coalinga pioneer, oilman, and inventor shows both the natural and "man-made" history of Coalinga. The land surrounding Coalinga is rich with oil and minerals and the museum emphasizes these assets. The oil is also responsible for the numerous well-preserved fossils found near here, including mastadon skeletons and an oil-preserved primeval lizard. Artifacts of the first men to live here, the Tachi tribe of the Yokut nation, include evidence that they used oil for trading. The crowded 1910 kitchen, 1880 advertising cards, collection of porcelain and glass insulators for telephone poles, and the doll collection are fascinating. Two of the most unusual treasures are 600 kinds of barbed wire dating from 1867 and a 1908 quilt made of silk swatches that were packed in Nebo cigarettes. There's even a "surrey with the fringe on top." The back room holds tools and machinery used in the oil fields.

Visitors to Coalinga will enjoy a drive nine miles north on Highways 33 and 198 past the Grasshopper oil pumps—oil field characters painted in many colors to look like clowns, birds, and animals.

TULARE COUNTY MUSEUM

Mooney Grove Park, Visalia. (209) 733-6616. Daily, 10–4; closed Tuesday and Wednesday in winter. Closed Tuesday in summer. 50¢.

"End of the Trail," the bronze sculpture by James Earl Fraser portraying a tired Indian on a pony—once the most copied piece of art in the world—is the star attraction at this lively museum. That sculpture was first exhibited in San Francisco in 1915 at the Panama-Pacific Exposition. A one-room schoolhouse, newspaper and dental office, and rooms from turn-of-the-century homes recreate the past. Furniture, clothes, cooking utensils, toys, baskets, World War I uniforms, and early farm machinery are also exhibited.

Outside, the 143-acre park offers picnic arbors under oak trees, boating, skateboard tracks, and more.

THE DEPOT RESTAURANT

207 East Oak Street, Railway Square, Visalia. (209) 732-8611. Lunch, 11:30–2:30; dinner, 5–10, until 11 on Friday and Saturday.

The old Visalia train station across the street from the museum is now a handsome restaurant with a railroad motif. At dinner, the "Caboose Special" (prime rib) and "Engineer's Delight" (steak and lobster) headline the bill.

BOYDEN CAVERN

Kings Canyon National Park, Highway 80 East of Fresno. (209) 736-2708. Daily, 10–5 June–September; daily, 11–4 May and October. Adults, $3.50; children, $1.75.

A 45-minute tour takes you into a wondrous world deep beneath the 2,000-foot-high marble walls of the famous Kings Gates. Massive stalagmites, delicate stalactites, and splendid arrays of crystalline formations defy description.

PORTERVILLE MUSEUM

257 North D Street, Porterville. (209) 784-9711. Thursday–Saturday, 10–5. Free.

The old Southern Pacific Railroad Station houses an interesting collection of historical artifacts of the Porterville pioneers. Included in displays are cameras, guns, saddles, stuffed and mounted animals indigenous to the area (including a California Condor), office equipment, glassware, and china. In other areas are a turn-of-the-century dining room, kitchen, pharmacy, and a good collection of American Indian basketry (primarily Yokuts). In the yard are old pieces of farming equipment and fire-engines plus a fully equipped blacksmith shop.

Also in Porterville, the Zalud House (Hockett and Morton; (209) 784-1400 ext. 604; Wednesday–Saturday, 10–4, Sunday, 2–4; adults 50¢, children 25¢) is an early residence completely furnished with original belongings of the Zalud family amid changing decor.

COLONEL ALLENSWORTH STATE HISTORIC PARK

Twenty miles north of Wasco on Highway 43, and nine miles west of Earlimart on Highway 99. Sotourna Avenue, Allensworth. (805) 849-3433.

The only California town to be founded, financed, and governed by Black Americans is being restored to its 1908 state. A visitor center with exhibits and films, picnic area, and two fully restored museums—the Colonel's residence and original schoolhouse—are open to the public upon request, as is the 15-unit campground. To schedule a tour write Star Route 1, Box 148, Allensworth, CA 93219.

SUN MAID RAISIN GROWERS

1325 South Bethel Avenue, off old Highway 99, Kingsburg. (209) 896-8000. Tours Monday–Friday, 10 A.M. and 1 P.M. Reservations advised.

Children of all ages are made most welcome here. Hostesses in Sun Maid costumes escort tours that begin with a 20-minute film on the production of raisins and end in the grower store. Visitors are also given samples to take home.

DISCOVERY CENTER

1944 North Winery Avenue, Fresno. (209) 251-5531. Tuesday–Saturday, 9:30–4; Sunday, 1–5. Adults, $1.25; ages 6–17, $1.25. Group rates. Astronomy program in summer.

This hands-on science center helps children try out things for themselves. There's a bubble machine, a chromium mirror, a tree that lights up by sound, a feel box, a reaction machine, and a peripheral-vision tester. The Indian room has a 100-year-old Yokut hut and shows the many things that the Indian has introduced to civilization such as tobacco, lacrosse, snowshoes, dyes, cranberries, pumpkins, turkey, cashews, and tomatoes. Dioramas of lake and valley birds are accompanied by questions to help you learn.

FORESTIERE UNDERGROUND GARDENS

5021 West Shaw Avenue (at Freeway 99), Fresno. (209) 275-3792. Tours every hour on the hour, June–September, 10–4, Wednesday–Sunday; weekends, holidays, and vacation time during the winter, weather permitting. Adults, $5; ages 13–17, $4; 5–12, $2.

Sicilian immigrant Baldasare Forestiere, a prosperous grapegrower and horticulturist, devoted his life to creating his own very individual way of life. When he decided that he couldn't bear the Fresno summer heat, he dug out a small underground room—and then kept digging until, forty years later, he had a seven-acre underground estate. Visitors wind through an amazing network of rooms, courts, patios, and passageways to view the strange and quite incredible fruit trees that Forestiere created. One tree grows seven fruits—Valencia and navel oranges, grapefruits, sweet and sour lemons, cheedro (a Sicilian rind fruit), and tangerines. Fig trees grow roots from one room to another and many more varieties—dates, pomegranates, loquats, carob trees, oriental jujubes, flowering quince, Italian pears—bend to the skylights. You'll also see Forestiere's living quarters and furnishings and the ponds in which he kept fish fresh for dinner. No one in our party finished the tour without admiration for a man who had a dream and who dedicated his life to achieving it.

Forestiere Gardens

BAR 20 DAIRY FARM

4260 West Madison Avenue, Fresno. (209) 264-0472. Daily 12–5. Guided tours by appointment. Free.

On your way to the Kearney mansion, stop off for a moment to see how cows are milked. The Bar 20 is a working farm, with one long gray building at the end of the driveway that is open to the public for "cow-viewing." One wall of the building is glass so you can see the cows as they line up to be washed, milked, fed, and corralled. A taped explanation tells you what's happening. In the corral outside, you can watch the calves at play.

FRESNO HISTORICAL SOCIETY MUSEUM AND M. THEO KEARNEY MANSION

7160 West Kearney Boulevard, Kearney Park, Fresno. (209) 441-0862. Thursday–Sunday, 1–4; weekends only in January and February. Adults, $2; ages 12–17, $1; under 12, 50¢.

M. Theodore Kearney, the first president of the California Raisin Growers Association, was a late nineteenth-century industrialist who lived and spent well. A guide takes you past hand-blown Tiffany lamps; photos of Mr. Kearney with his luxurious cars and his old flame, Lillie Langtry; and his office safe with a floor of concrete five feet thick. A Mother Goose book, 1908 dictionary, feather bed, and shelf of toys are in the nursery. Listen to the piano roll in the dining room and note the buzzer on the arm of Kearney's chair, which was used to page the servants. The fully furnished bedrooms with clothes laid out make a visitor feel that the Kearneys have just stepped out and will be back any moment. The mansion is set in a lovely park with a tea house, playgrounds, and picnic areas.

ROEDING PARK ZOO AND STORYLAND

890 West Belmont, Roeding Park, Fresno. Zoo: (209) 488-1549 and 264-5988. Daily, 10–5; til 8 in summer. Over 15 years, $1.50. Storyland: 264-2235. Daily 10–5 in summer; weekends in winter; closed December and January. Over 3 years, $1. The park is open from 10–5 daily.

More than 668 birds, mammals, and reptiles live in this neat little zoo. The aviary is green and open, with a walkway that allows you to see the birds "head-on." The door to the giraffes' shelter is marked with a scale of feet and inches so you can measure how tall the giraffes are. There are rare white rhinos, orangutans with babies, and a scimitar-horned oryx. You can peek into the nursery through a glass window.

In Storyland, talking storybook keys ($1) persuade the blue caterpillar to tell eight classic fairytales; when the children have heard the stories, they can go on to visit the heroes of the tales. They can play in King Arthur's castle, Red Riding Hood's grandmother's cottage, Mr. Toad's cart, or they can talk to Simple Simon's pie man, the knights and knaves of Alice's court, the Three Bears, or Little Miss Muffet. They can follow the Crooked Mile, slide down Jack's beanstalk, climb Owl's tree, and have a drink at Mother Goose's fountain.

Fort Millerton (488-1551, 10–5 weekends, donation) is an old block house that now has an exhibit of pioneer life. Visitors can see antique children's toys, the history of the lumber industry, and the complete medical kit of Fresno's first doctor.

SAN JOAQUIN FISH HATCHERY

Friant, off Highway 41, 13 miles northeast of Fresno. (209) 822-2374. 8–4:30 daily. Free.

There are more fish in this one spot than you'll ever see again: more than two million trout in sizes that range from pinhead to fingerling to almost catchable are raised in these trout-hatching ponds. Four times a day the fish are fed high-protein, dry pellets. When they're a year old and ten inches long, they're taken in tanks by plane and truck to the heavily fished lakes and streams of California. But while they're here, it's really fun to walk along the forty-eight ponds and watch the fish leap over and slide down the little dams between them. A photo exhibit explains trout habits and the trout-seeding program.

FRIANT DAM AND MILLERTON LAKE STATE RECREATIONAL AREA

Off Highway 41. (209) 822-2212. Daily, 9–3. $2 per car to enter park.

Fed by Sierra snows, the waters of Millerton Lake are released into the Friant-Kern irrigation canals to feed the rich croplands of Fresno County. The dam is 319 feet high and 3,488 feet long with a reservoir capacity of 5.2 million gallons. You can walk halfway across the dam while guides tell you the history of the project. Millerton Lake State Recreation Area offers boating, swimming, fishing, camping, and picnic space. The old Millerton Courthouse, overlooking the dam, is a pleasant little museum of Friant history (by appointment, 822-2332).

Friant Dam

MADERA COUNTY MUSEUM

210 West Yosemite, Madera. (209) 673-0291. Weekends 1–4 and by appointment. Free.

Three floors of displays emphasize the county's mining, logging, and agricultural history, in the 1900 granite courthouse set in the city park. The Superior Courtroom has been restored and there's a section of the flume of the Madera Sugar Pine Lumber Company. The "downtown room" shows what the city looked like in 1900 and even has a real stagecoach.

FRESNO FLATS HISTORIC PARK

Highway 427, Oakhurst. (209) 683-7463. Saturday and Sunday, 1–4. Adults, $1; children, 50¢.

The Sierra Historic Sites Association has restored the 111-year-old Marge Lyman home and the original Fresno Flats Schoolhouse is being converted into the Nathan Sweet Museum to tell the story of the area and its people. A 20' x 40' log house from 1869 is being restored.

MARIPOSA COUNTY HISTORY CENTER

Highway 140 at Tenth Street, Mariposa. (209) 966-2924. Daily 10–5; weekends only in winter. Donation.

Inside, you'll find an 1850s street, with newspaper office, assay office, saloon, drug store, and 1850s schoolroom, each furnished as it was in Gold Rush days. A five-stamp mill that crushed gold-bearing quartz at the Golden Key mine, a hand-operated Washington Hoe printing press, and a reconstructed Indian village will enthrall inquiring youngsters.

The nearby Mariposa County Courthouse (966-2005, Monday–Friday 9–5; tours by appointment and weekend tours 10–5 April–October; free) is the oldest courthouse still in use in California. The clock in the tower has been counting time since 1866. Visitors will enjoy the "law in motion" days on the second and fourth Friday of each month and the extensive collection of Mariposa County gemstones and minerals in the halls.

The Mariposa Jail nearby now houses the magnificent collection of the California Division of Mines and Geology Mineral Exhibit that used to be in San Francisco's Ferry Building.

YOSEMITE MOUNTAIN SUGAR PINE RAILROAD

Highway 41, Yosemite Mountain, Fish Camp. (209) 683-7273. Daily 10–4 in summer; weekends and holidays, weather permitting in September and May; closed November through April. Adults $5.75; ages 3-12, $3.25.

Just four miles from Yosemite Basin, this scenic, historic narrow-gauge steam railroad and logging train wends its way through four miles of forest, past Slab Town Loop and Honey Hill and down to the bottom of a canyon. You can stop there and have a picnic and then return on a later train.

YOSEMITE NATIONAL PARK

Enter through Fish Camp on Highway 41, El Portal on Highway 140, or Highway 120 (this road to Tioga Pass is closed during the winter, which may last until May). Visitor's Center: (209) 372-4461. Daily, 8–6; 9–5 in spring and fall; winter weekends, weather permitting. Museum open daily in summer only. Cars $3 a day.

If you and your family had only one sight to see in California, your best choice would be Yosemite National Park. Yosemite is one of the world's wonders and is a world within itself for both man and nature. Elevations range from less than 2,000 to over 13,000 feet and, in these 11,000 feet, five different plant belts exist. Each sustains a part of the park's wildlife population of 220 bird and 75 mammal species. In this natural splendor you can hike, swim, camp, fish, ski, ride horseback, bicycle, or simply go sightseeing. Your first stop should be the Visitors Center in Yosemite Valley where you can learn about the park from the center's pamphlets, exhibits, audiovisual programs, lectures, and guided walks. The *Yosemite Guide,* free, at entrance stations, gives the latest schedules. One program complete with fireside stories and toasted marshmallows was created especially for youngsters.

Where you go in Yosemite will, of course, depend on your time, interests, and the time of year. You can choose from mountains, giant sequoia

Yosemite Mountain Sugar Pine Railroad

groves, towering waterfalls like Bridal Veil, and breathtaking vistas of Sentinel Rock and El Capitan.

There are also museums in Yosemite for rainy days or a change of pace. The Indian Cultural Center near the Visitors Center is of interest. Be sure to go through the self-guiding reconstruction of the Ahwaneechee Indian Village, 9–12:45, 2–5:30 daily. At the Pioneer Yosemite History Center at Wawona you can wander through a collection of horse-drawn vehicles, an old jail, a miner's hut, a working wagon shop, and a covered bridge. Old-time crafts demonstrations of soap-making, rail-splitting, and spinning are fun, and you can talk to costumed historian-interpreters who portray the original occupants of cabins representing the different stages in the development of Yosemite National Park.

The Yosemite Travel Museum, in the Administration area near Arch Rock entrance, tells the story of early-day railroad and auto transportation in the Yosemite region. It has a caboose, a locomotive, and a couple of cars on the grounds. The *Geology Museum* at the Visitors Center in Yosemite Valley, shows how the mountains, waterfalls, and gorges in Yosemite were formed. The natural history of Yosemite is also explored at the *Happy Isles Nature Center.*

Yosemite is always very crowded in July and August, so it is wise to plan your visit during June or September, if you can. For information about the park, write to Superintendent, Yosemite National Park, CA 95389, or telephone (209) 372-4461. Camp reservations may be made through Ticketron. Hotel reservations are a must. Call 373-4171 or contact the Yosemite Park and Curry Co., Yosemite National Park, CA 95389. For road and weather information, call 372-4605.

BODIE STATE HISTORIC PARK

13 miles east of Highway 395; seven miles south of Bridgeport; Bodie. Accessible only in summer. Smoking is allowed in designated areas only. Free.

Nestled high in sagebrush country, Bodie has escaped all the commercialism found in most ghost towns of the West—it doesn't even have a phone. The 170 original buildings that still stand are maintained in a state of arrested disintegration—neither restored nor allowed to decay further. You walk by the 1878 Methodist church, the windowless jail, a frame schoolhouse, a small home that belonged to President Hoover's brother, the morgue with caskets still on view, and the iron vault of the bank, which was the scene of many exciting holdups. Information comes from a self-guiding tour pamphlet stowed in a container on the side of a building. Just wander through this quiet, ramshackle town and imagine all the high adventures that occurred here, more than a century ago.

NORTH CENTRAL CALIFORNIA

The north central and northeastern area is the most rugged, remote part of Northern California, yet offers many unique and extraordinary sights. Lava Beds National Monument, Modoc National Forest, and Lassen Volcanic National Park are snowed-in in winter and blazingly hot in summer. Distances between towns are long, so be sure to arrange overnight camping or lodging before you set out. Nature lovers will enjoy the Whiskeytown–Lake Shasta–Trinity area and McArthur Burney Falls Memorial State Park—and all the wonderful open spaces whose very inaccessibility makes them places to aim for.

COMMUNITY MEMORIAL MUSEUM

1333 Butte House Road, Yuba City. (916) 674-0461. Monday–Friday, 9–5; Saturday, 1–4. Free.

This small community museum houses artifacts of the Indians and early pioneers of Sutter County, as well as exhibits on the natural history of the area. Baskets, beads, and grinding pots represent the local Indians, while antique pianos lugged around Cape Horn, family books and bibles, and everyday clothing and dishes depict pioneer life. Mementos from the Chinese settlers are also included. But the starring item in the collection is Lola Montez' dressing table, surely one of the "tools" of this dazzling actress and seductress.

In Marysville, Yuba's Sister City, an 1857 family residence has become a museum, the *Mary Aaron Memorial Museum* (704 D Street, Tuesday–Saturday, 1:30–4:30 P.M., tours by appointment for fourth graders and older; free; (916) 743-1004) with the original furniture and clothing and an interesting display of dolls, documents, and photographs. Our favorite artifact is an 1860s wedding cake that was discovered perfectly intact and petrified in a wooden Wells Fargo storage box.

SACRAMENTO VALLEY MUSEUM

1495 E Street, Highway 20 at Interstate 5, Williams. (916) 473-2978. Summer:

Friday–Wednesday, 10–5; Sunday, 1–5. Winter: Friday, Saturday, 10–5; Sunday, 1–5. Adults, $1; ages 6–16, 25¢.

A general store, a blacksmith shop and saddlery, an apothecary shop, a barber shop, and restored early California rooms are included in this twenty-one-room museum that is filled with memories. The doll collection dates from Mycenaean times and there's even an 1800 newspaper reporting President George Washington's death. The double cradle from the 1700s is also special.

OROVILLE CHINESE TEMPLE

1500 Broderick, Oroville. (916) 533-1496. Friday–Tuesday, 10–12 and 1–4:30 in winter, also 1–4:30 Wednesday and Thursday in summer. Ages 12 and older, $1.50, tours of 15 or more, $1 each.

This complex of Buddhist, Taoist, and Confucian temples houses one of the finest collections of Chinese artifacts in the United States. At the door of one building stands a two-ton, cast-iron urn given to the temple by Emperor Quong She. Carved teakwood altars, old tapestries, gods and goddesses, dragons, rare lanterns, and shrines are found throughout the buildings. The Moon Temple, used for Buddhist worship is entered through a circular doorway, which symbolizes the circle of life. The arts and lives of the thousands of Chinese who migrated to the gold fields are wonderfully reflected in this peaceful spot.

Nearby is the *Lott House Museum* at 1607 Montgomery Street (916/533-7699; same hours as Chinese Temple, $1). Once the home of Judge C. F. Lott, this nineteenth-century house is furnished with period pieces and early American art.

The *Oroville Pioneer Museum,* further up Montgomery Street (916/534-0198; 1–4 Sunday and by appointment; donation) is a grand collection of pioneer memorabilia including early typewriters, an old fire engine, pictures of the Oroville floods, and a facsimile miner's cabin.

FEATHER RIVER FISH HATCHERY AND OROVILLE DAM

5 Table Mountain Boulevard, Oroville. (916) 534-2465. Hatchery: 8–6 daily. Dam overlook (534-2324): 8 A.M.–9 P.M. May–September; 8–8 October and November; 8–5 December–April. Free.

A large window in the hatchery enables visitors to see the salmon climb the fish ladder to spawn (usually in September). Over 10,000 salmon and steelhead make their homes here now. Ten miles up the road, you can get a good view of the 770-foot dam across the Feather River.

BIDWELL MANSION

525 Esplanade, Chico. (916) 895-6144. Daily, 10–4, except holidays. 45 minute guided tours every hour on the hour. Adults, 50¢.

Rancho del Arroyo Chico, covering 26,000 acres, was purchased in 1849 by agriculturalist and politician John Bidwell. His large Victorian home soon became the social and cultural center of the upper Sacramento Valley. Bidwell's is a California success story. He arrived in California in 1841, worked as a clerk for John Sutter, served as an officer in the Mexican War, and then on July fourth, 1848, made a gold strike at Bidwell Bar. After that, he set himself up at Chico and built a model farm. He raised corn, oats, barley, peaches, pears, apples, figs, quince, almonds, walnuts, wheat, olives, and casaba melons. He was elected state senator and congressman, and even ran for President. Visitors may walk through the graciously furnished rooms. Children will like the cabinet of stuffed birds in the General's office and the intricate Victorian hair wreaths in the parlor. Bidwell Park, fourth largest municipal park in the nation, was also part of the Bidwell estate.

The nearby *Stansbury Home* (Fifth and Salem; 343-4401 ext. 236; Saturday and Sunday, 1–4; adults 75¢, children 50¢), an 1883 Italianate Victorian filled with period furnishings, is remarkable because only Stansburys have lived in it and it has never been remodeled or modernized.

Bidwell Mansion

SOUTH SHASTA LINES

G.A. Humann Ranch, 8620 Holmes Road, Gerber. (916) 385-1389. Open even-numbered years in April and May on Sunday from 12–3. Adults, $3; under 12, $2.

A one-quarter-inch scale model railroad representing the Southern Pacific, Gerber to Dunsmuir, built during 34 years by the Humann family, runs 15 steam locomotives and 100 cars on an 840-foot track. There are 1,200 miniature trees, 700 people, and 200 animals on this detailed miniature system. In addition, a real steam locomotive and train take visitors for a mile-long ride. On Saturday and Sunday of Labor Day weekend, during odd-numbered years, the Humanns present an Old Time Steam Threshing Bee (same price). This operating display and demonstration of threshing, plowing, baling, and milling is a family show not to be missed.

WILLIAM B. IDE ADOBE

1 mile north of Red Bluff on Adobe Road. (916) 527-5927. 8–5 daily; adobe open 12–4. Free.

"He hereby invites all good and patriotic citizens in California to assist him—to establish and perpetuate a liberal, a just and honorable government, which shall secure to all civil, religious and personal liberty." So wrote William B. Ide to introduce the Bear Flag Republic to California. As first President of the Bear Flag Republic, he helped bring California into the Union. But when the Republic failed, Ide went to the gold fields and then returned home to his adobe, which also served as a ferry station between Sacramento and Shasta's Northern Gold Mines. The house is small and unassuming, with family photos, cradle and high chair, a furnished kitchen, and an unusual sleeping platform under the eaves. A smokehouse and a carriage house, with covered wagons, buggies, and Ide's branding equipment, are also open to the public. Two 300-year-old oaks lead the way to another small museum that includes gold-mining tools, an old button collection and a well-used cribbage board.

In Red Bluff, the Kelly-Griggs House Museum (311 Washington Street, 527-1129) is open for old house buffs, Thursday–Sunday, 2–5. Donation.

RED BLUFF DAM AND RECREATION AREA

End of Williams Avenue and Sale Lane, Red Bluff. (916) 527-3248. Dawn to dusk daily. Free.

Closed-circuit cameras and interpretive exhibits on chinook salmon relate the story of the king salmon, largest of the five Pacific salmon species. Fish trapping, camping, picnicking, and boat launch are available.

Salmon Spawning Channels (2 miles south of Red Bluff, Route 99 West, east of Tyler Road; (916) 527-7440; 8–8:30 daily, free), one of the world's largest and most technically advanced man-made salmon spawning channels, feature a visitors kiosk and overlook with interpretive exhibits on chinook salmon. A view of naturally spawning salmon is possible October through November.

Fish hatchery buffs might like to ride to Anderson, six miles off Highway 5, above Red Bluff, to see the Coleman National Fish Hatchery (365-8622, 8–4:30 daily, free), the world's largest chinook salmon plant. Every year up to 14 million salmon and steelhead trout are raised and released into Battle Creek. Spawning takes place in the fall, but there's always something to see here. For information on other hatcheries in California, call (916) 275-1589.

CARTER HOUSE SCIENCE MUSEUM

Caldwell Park, 1701 Rio Drive, Redding. (916) 225-4125. Wednesday–Sunday, 12–4. Free.

Did you know that tarantulas enjoy walking along your arm? In the petting section of this lively junior science museum, you can pet a tarantula—or a possum or ground squirrel. Native animals that are injured—sparrow hawks, screech owls, California boa constrictors—and domestic animals are cared for here. Free nature and science films on weekends and special programs such as moon rock displays keep the place jumping.

REDDING MUSEUM AND ART CENTER

1911 Rio Drive, Caldwell Park, Redding. (916) 225-4155. Daily 10–5, except Monday in summer; Tuesday–Friday and Sunday, 12–5 and Saturday, 10–5 in winter; closed holidays. Free.

A fantastic doll collection is just one of the many revolving exhibits in this excellent museum. Carousel animals is another, as are changing historical exhibits. The story of Pomo Indian basketry—from cradle, to pots, dresses, luggage, and houses to gifts for the funeral pyre—is remarkable. The permanent Indian and primitive collections include pre-Columbian pottery, canoe prows from the Trobriand Islands, and "wife beaters" from the Australian aborigines. Crafts and baskets from the Hoopa, Karok, Yurok, Wintu, Zuni, Yaqui, and Hopi Indians are nicely presented. The art galleries also offer constantly changing exhibits of contemporary artists. Recent shows have focused on Amish quilts; scarecrows; and California artist Bruce Conner.

SHASTA

Highway 299 west of Redding, Old Shasta. (916) 243-8194. Daily 10–5. Adults, 50¢; ages 6–17, 25¢.

Once the center of the rich northern gold mines, Shasta is now a quiet ghost town in the process of being restored. The old county courthouse contains a remarkable collection of California art along with displays of photographs and relics of the Indians, Chinese, gold miners, and pioneers who once lived here. Modoc handicrafts, Chinese wooden pillows and money, an 1879 *Godey's Ladies Book*, and the pistol John Brown used in his raid at Harper's Ferry are a few of the highlights. The courtroom is furnished as it was when in use and the jail is still equipped with chains, leg irons, and a gallows. The Litsch Miners' Supply Store, open in summer, looks just as it did in the 1860s, with barrels of meat and wine, old hats, and picks and shovels for sale. Picnic areas are available near the barn and stagecoach.

J. J. (JAKE) JACKSON MEMORIAL MUSEUM AND TRINITY COUNTY HISTORICAL PARK

Main Street, Highway 299 West, Weaverville. (916) 623-5211. Daily, 10–5 May–November. Free.

Museum displays trace Trinity County's history from the days of the Indian through the gold-mining years. Ray Jackson's collection of antique firearms, Chinese tong war weapons, and reconstructed miner's cabin and blacksmith shop help to recall this bygone era.

WEAVERVILLE CHINESE JOSS HOUSE

Highway 299 West, Weaverville. (916) 623-5284. Daily 10–5, except holidays. Adults, 50¢.

Tours every hour on the hour in winter, on the half hour in summer. The Temple of the Forest and the Clouds is open for worship now, as it has been since 1853. A small museum displays Chinese art, mining tools, weapons used in the tong wars, and photos of Chinese laborers building the railroads. A Lion Dance headdress, an abacus, opium pipes, and a huge gong are also shown. Inside the temple, you see the paper money that is burned for the gods and the drum and bell that wake the gods so they'll hear your prayers. In the rear of the temple, the attendants' quarters are furnished as they were one hundred years ago, with bunk beds and wooden pillows. Colorful altars, temple saints, celebration drums and flags, and the mirror-covered king's umbrella that guarded him against evil spirits create a vivid picture of the religion and its people.

IRONSIDE MUSEUM

Hawkins Bar, on Highway 299 West near Burnt Ranch. (916) 629-2396. By chance or by appointment. Donation.

Ray Nachand shares his personal collection daily in summer and irregularly in winter. Pioneer artifacts include butter churns, doctor's instruments, guns, a collection of two hundred padlocks, a glass insulator collection, Mrs. Nachand's carnival glass collection, and high-button shoes. Assaying equipment, mining equipment, machinery, and a blacksmith shop share the bill with gold that Mr. Nachand has mined.

HOOPA TRIBAL MUSEUM

Hoopa Valley Indian Reservation, Highway 96 (off 299 West), Hoopa. (916) 625-4110. Monday–Friday, 9–5:30 in winter, Saturday also in summer. Free.

Stone implements, dishes, tools, baskets, and dance regalia of the Hoopa Indians—named by Jedediah Smith's Yurok guide as "the people who live up the river"—are shown here, along with items from other tribes such as Kachina dolls from the Southwest, and Alaskan and Canadian baskets. Many of the Hoopa items are on loan from local residents in a living museum of artifacts used regularly in traditional tribal ceremonies as part of a living culture.

SHASTA DAM

Highway 15 off Interstate 5. (916) 275-1587. Daily 9–5 in summer; films daily at 10, 12, and 2 in winter. Free.

Deer come to be fed by children when the lights shine on Shasta Dam at night. During the day, the 602-foot dam, second highest in the world, is an even more spectacular sight. Snow-capped Mount Shasta (which is climbable) looms in the distance, accentuating the differences between natural and man-made wonders. A self-guided tour and a model and film explain

Weaverville Chinese Joss House

how the dam works. Jet-boat tours, houseboating, and every kind of water
sport are popular in this Whiskeytown–Shasta–Trinity National Recreation
Area. Scott's Museum, in Trinity Center is open daily 10–5 in summer and
features items of local history.

LAKE SHASTA CAVERNS

*Off Lake Shasta in O'Brien. (916) 238-2341. Two-hour tours throughout the day, in-
cluding a 15-minute catamaran ride across the lake, from 8 A.M. in summer, 10–2 in
winter. Adults, $7; children 5-15, $3.*

   Discovered in 1878 by J. A. Richardson (you can still see his inscription),
the Lake Shasta Caverns are a natural wonder. Stalactite and stalagmite
formations range from the eight-inch high "Ballerina" to the sixty-foot
"Cathedral Room" of stalactite draperies that are studded with crystals. Mul-
ticolored formations unfold before you during your tour, as you hear fact
and Wintu Indian legend from a knowledgeable guide.

SISKIYOU COUNTY MUSEUM

Old Shasta lives again!

910 South Main Street, Yreka. (916) 842-3836. Monday–Saturday 9–5 in summer,
Tuesday–Saturday in winter. Free.

In this reproduction of the Callahan Ranch Hotel, one of the first stage stops in Siskiyou County in the 1850s, visitors will learn the story of Siskiyou County from prehistoric days to the present. On the mezzanine you'll find a parlor, bedroom, children's room, and office complete with an antique switchboard. In the basement you'll see a country store, milliner's shop, music store, blacksmith shop, miner's cabin, and tools. A schoolhouse, blacksmith shop, church, 1856 pioneer log cabin, ore car, and logging skid shack are on the grounds along with many farming implements. A trip to this museum is a trip to the past.

Nearby, The County Court House at Fourth and Lane Streets (916/842-3531; Monday–Friday, 8–5) displays gold nuggets, panned gold, placer gold, and local gemstones.

LAVA BEDS NATIONAL MONUMENT

Off Highway 139, near Tule Lake. (916) 667-2282. Camping, $6 in summer only.

Natural and Indian history vie for the visitor's attention in this monumental landscape created by black lava from the earth's crust. The area abounds with natural wonders, including cinder cones that reach up as high as five hundred feet. Lava running underground has shaped hundreds of caves which can be explored with care. The Merrill Ice Caves contain a still river and a waterfall formed of ice. Another is decorated with drawings by the Indians who once lived here. Captain Jack's Stronghold, a fort fashioned of lava, is a grim reminder of later history: In 1872, Captain Jack led a band of Modoc Indians in a bloody but unsuccessful uprising against the U.S. Cavalry. This was the only Indian war in California. A short visit to monument headquarters (open 8–5 in summer, 8–4:30 when weather permits in winter) will help you understand the geology, natural history, and past events of the area.

ALTURAS MODOC COUNTY HISTORICAL MUSEUM

600 South Main, Alturas. (916) 233-2944. May 1–November 1, 9–4 weekdays, 10–
4:30 weekends and Christmas week. Free.

To learn more about Captain Jack and see pictures of him, go to this pleasant museum in the far corner of the state. There are beads, baskets, arrowheads, and other Indian artifacts along with pioneer memorabilia. The collections of mounted animals and birds and antique guns are visitors' favorites.

ROOPS' FORT

75 North Weatherlow Street, Susanville. (916) 257-5721. Daily 10–4, May 15–

November 15. Free.

Lassen County memorabilia; farming and lumbering machinery; artifacts of the native Americans; and remembrances of the first settlers, Isaac Roops and Peter Lassen, fill this interesting museum. You can peek through the fence of next-door Roops' Fort, built in 1854, the first in Lassen County, to see wagon wheels from the Donner Party. Susanville is named after the daughter of Isaac Roops, Governor of the Provisional Territory of Nevada and Nataqua.

LASSEN VOLCANIC NATIONAL PARK

Highway 36, Mineral. (916) 595-4444. Information centers at Manzanita Lake and Sulphur Works open from early June to late September. Road closed in winter.

Caves, hot springs, boiling pools, mud pots, sparkling lakes, and the cinder cone that erupted in 1851 are visitor attractions in this rugged area. An Indian lore program at park headquarters tells the story and customs of the Yana, Yahi, Mountain Maidu, and Atsugewi Indians who once lived here. Ishi, story-book hero and last man of the Yahi tribe, was found near here and the photos of him living with his customs in a modern world are interesting. Indians of other tribes still sell baskets and tell stories on the campgrounds. One note of warning: The grounds and thermal areas are treacherous, so keep hold of your children at all times. Lassen Peak erupted for seven years beginning in May 1914 and it's due for another blow soon.

PUBLIC RELATIONS TOURS

RUMIANO CHEESE CO.   *Country Road F, Willows. (916) 934-5438.* Tours, arranged by appointment, will see the packaging and cutting of huge dry jack wheels, Monterey Jack, pepper jack, and seven other cheeses.

———————

SPECIAL ANNUAL EVENTS

JANUARY

San Francisco Sports and Boat Show, Cow Palace.

San Mateo Auto Show, Fairgrounds.

Harlem Globe Trotters, Oakland Coliseum.

Golden Gate Kennel Club All-Breed Dog Show, San Francisco.

Four-Dog Sled Races, Prosser Lake and Donner Lake.

Whale watching begins, Pt. Reyes National Seashore.

Fiddler's Contest and Crab Cioppino Feed, Cloverdale.

FEBRUARY

Chinese New Years Celebration, San Francisco.

Athens Track Meet.

National Road Show, Oakland Coliseum.

Crab Festival, Crescent City.

Crab Cioppino Feast, Bodega Bay.

Redwood Region Logging Conference, Eureka.

Chinese Bomb Day, Bok Kai Festival, Marysville.

Cloverdale Citrus Fair (third weekend).

Clam Beach Run, Trinidad.

Carnival and Spring Fair, Lakeport.

California Special Olympics Winter Games, Sonora.

MARCH

Snowfest, Lake Tahoe.

Camellia Show, Santa Rosa.

Crab Feed, Ukiah.

Draggin' Wagins Dance Festival, Sonora.

Sierra Dog Sled Races, Sierra City, Truckee and Ebbets Pass.

Candlefishing at Night, Klamath River.

Fresno Camellia Show.

Junior Grand National Livestock Expo, Cow Palace, San Francisco.

Jackass Mail Run, Porterville (or first weekend in April).

Cherry Blossom Festival, Japantown, San Francisco (or early April).

Dandelion Days Fair, Jackson.

Mendocino Coast Whale Festival.

APRIL

Log Race, Petaluma River.

Fisherman's Festival, Bodega Bay.

Baseball season opens.

Annual Trinidad Crab Feed.

Gem and Mineral Show, Cow Palace, San Francisco.

Yacht Parade, Redwood City.

Clovis Rodeo.

Carmel Kite Festival.

Gold Nugget Days, Paradise.

Children's Lawn Festival,
Redding.
Red Bluff Romp and Rodeo.
Coalinga Water Festival.
Nikkei Matsuri Festival, San
Jose.
Apple Blossom Festival, Sebas-
topol.
Fresno Folk Festival.
Rhododendron Festival,
Eureka.
Boonville Buck-A-Roo Days.
Calaveras County Jumping
Frog Jubilee, Angels Camp.
Motherlode Dixieland Jazz
Festival.

MAY

Laguna Seca Races, Monterey.
Cinco de Mayo Festivals in San
Francisco and San Jose.
Opening Day Yacht Parade, San
Francisco.
Ferndale Arts Festival.
Avenue of the Giants
Marathon, Garberville.
Bay to Breakers Race, San
Francisco.
Luther Burbank Rose Festival,
Santa Rosa.
Mendocino Art Fair.
Mt. Folk Festival, Potter Valley.
West Coast National Antique
Fly-In, Watsonville Airport.
Salinas Valley Fair, King City.
West Coast Relays, Fresno.
Chamarita Festival and Parade,
Half Moon Bay (Pentecost
Sunday).
Chamarita Festival and Parade,
Sausalito (Pentecost Sunday).
Old Settlers Day, Campbell.
Fireman's Muster, Columbia.
Lamb Derby Days, Willow.
Russian River Wine Festival,
Healdsburg.

Stump Town Days and Rodeo,
Guerneville (or early June).
Coarsegold Rodeo, Madera
County.
Fiddletown Gold Country
Hoedown.
Prospector's Daze, Willow
Creek.

JUNE

Black Bart Celebration, Red-
wood Valley.
Sonoma/Marin Fair, Petaluma
Fairgrounds.
Upper Grant Avenue Street
Fair, San Francisco.
Fly-In and Moonlight Flight,
Porterville.
Alameda County Fair,
Pleasanton.
Merienda, Monterey's birthday
party.
San Antonio Mission Fiesta,
Jolon.
Springfest, San Mateo Fair-
grounds.
Old Auburn Flea Market.
Italian Picnic and Parade, Sut-
ter Creek.
Klamath Salmon barbecue.
Shasta Brigade Jamboree,
Redding.
Malakoff Home-Coming,
Nevada City.
Solano County Fair, Vallejo.
Novato County Fair.
Pony Express Days, McKin-
leyville.
Garberville Rodeo and Western
Celebration.
San Francisco Kite Festival.
Bear Flag Day, Sonoma.
Tuolumne Jubilee, Tuolumne
City.
Days of Kit Carson, Jackson.
Butterfly Days, Mariposa.
Cornish Miner's Picnic, Grass
Valley.

Fiddler's Jamboree, Railroad
Flat.
Bonanza Days, Gilroy.
Redwood Acres Fair, Eureka.
Western Daze, Fairfield.
Western Weekend, Novato.
Vaquero Days, Hollister.
Horse Show and Rodeo, San
Benito.
Midsummer Music Festival, Sig-
mund Stern Grove, San Fran-
cisco (through August).
Highway 50 Wagon Train,
Placerville.
Secession Day, Rough and
Ready (June 27).
San Francisco's Birthday
Celebration.
Russian River Rodeo and
Stumptown Days, Guerne-
ville.

JULY

Old Time Fourth of July
Celebration, Columbia.
Salmon B-B-Q, Noyo.
Sonoma County Fair, Santa
Rosa.
C.B. Radio Convention,
Eureka.
Bach Festival, Carmel.
California Rodeo, Salinas.
Nihon Machi Street Fair, San
Francisco.
Asian Festival, Oakland
Museum.
Hoopa Fourth of July Celebra-
tion.
Pony Express Celebration, Pol-
lack Pines.
Napa County Fair, Calistoga
(July Fourth).
Willits Frontier Days (Fourth of
July).
Arcata Salmon Festival.
Mendota Sugar Jamboree.
Garberville Rodeo.
San Mateo County Fair.

Woodminster Music Series,
Oakland (through Septem-
ber).
San Francisco Fair and Exposi-
tion.
Hangtown Festival, Placerville.
Sacramento Water Festival.
Old-Fashioned Fourth, Mt.
Shasta.
Old-Fashioned Fourth, Cres-
cent City.
Dune Daze, Samoa.
Grand Comedy Festival,
Eureka.
Fortuna Rodeo.
Water Carnival, Monte Rio.
Jeepers Jamboree, Georgetown
to Lake Tahoe.
Fiesta Rodeo de San Juan
Bautista.
Captain Weber Days, Stockton.
Obon Festival, Monterey.
Obon Festival, Fresno.
Scotts Valley Days.
Gold Rush Jubilee, Callahan,
Siskiyou County.
Feast of Lanterns, Pacific
Grove.
Orick Rodeo.
Easter Lily Festival, Smith River.
Gasket Raft Races.
Turtle Races, Cloverdale.
Nightboat Parade, Lakeport
and Clearlake Highlands.

AUGUST

Old Adobe Days, Petaluma.
Monterey County Fair.
Humboldt County Fair, Fern-
dale.
Dipsea Foot Race, Mill Valley.
California State Horseman's
American Horse Show,
Sonoma.
"Annie and Mary Day," Blue
Lake.
Santa Clara County Fair, San
Jose.

Gilroy Garlic Festival.
Wildwood Days and Peddlers'
   Faire, Rio Dell.
Siskiyou County Fair and Paul
   Bunyan Jubilee.
Ringling Brothers Circus, Oak-
   land.
Calamari Festival, Santa Cruz.
Jamestown Pioneer Days.
El Dorado Days at Mt. Ranch,
   San Andreas.
Mother Lode Fair and Loggers'
   Contest, Sonora.
Plumas County Fair, Quincy.
Pony Express Day, McKinley-
   ville (August 22).
Children's Fairyland Birthday
   Week, Oakland.
Air Round-Up, Red Bluff.
Willow Creek Bigfoot Days.
Del Norte County Fair, Crescent
   City.
Gravenstein Apple Fair, Sebas-
   topol.
Lake County Fair, Lakeport.
Marin County Fair, San Rafael.

SEPTEMBER

Sausalito Art Festival.
Begonia Festival, Capitola.
Monterey Jazz Festival.
Renaissance Faire, Novato.
Mendocino County Fair and
   Apple Show, Boonville.
Ringling Brothers Circus, San
   Francisco.
San Francisco Art Festival.
Fall Festival, Japantown, San
   Francisco.
Redwood Empire Logging Fes-
   tival, McKinleyville.
Constitution Days, Nevada City.
Vintage Festival, Hall of Flow-
   ers, Golden Gate Park, San
   Francisco.
California State Fair, Sac-
   ramento.
Scottish Games, Santa Rosa
   Fairgrounds.

Pageant of Fire Mountain,
   Guerneville.
Vintage Car Fair, Fremont.
National Indian Observance
   Day, Crescent City.
American Indian Day, Volcano.
Paul Bunyan Days, Fort Bragg.
Concord Jazz Festival.
Indian "Big Time" Days, Ama-
   dor County.
Capitola Begonia Festival.
Santa Cruz County Fair, Wat-
   sonville.
Salinas Rodeo.
Vintage Festival, Sonoma.
Northcountry Fair, Arcata.
Carmel Mission Fiesta.
Fiesta del Pueblo, San Jose.
Redwood Invitational Regatta,
   Big Lagoon, Humboldt
   County.
Oktoberfest, San Mateo Fair-
   grounds.
Oktoberfest, San Jose.
Lodi Grape Festival.
Fiesta Patrias, Woodland.
Castroville Artichoke Festival.
Walnut Festival, Walnut Creek.
Sonoma Valley of the Moon Fes-
   tival.
Sourdough days, Sutter Hill.

OCTOBER

Laguna Seca Grand Prix, Mon-
   terey.
Fortuna Arts Festival.
Sonoma County Harvest Fes-
   tival, Santa Rosa.
Fresno Fair.
National Livestock Expo, San
   Francisco.
Marin Grape Festival, San
   Rafael.
Pumpkin Festival, Half Moon
   Bay.
Football season starts.
Spanishtown Art and Pumpkin
   Festival.

Candle Lighter Ghost House,
Fremont.
Pro-Am Surfing International,
Santa Cruz.
Redding Children's Art Festival.
Fall Festival, Clearlake Oaks.
Selma Parade and Band Festival.
Blessing of the Fleet, San Francisco.

Johnny Appleseed Day, Paradise.
Lumberjack Day, West Point.
Harbor Festival, Morro Bay.
Great Sandcastle Building Contest, Carmel.
Great Snail Race, Folsom.
Octoberfest, Tahoe City.
Old Timers' Day, King City.
Columbus Day Festival, San Carlos.

Octoberfest—San Mateo Fairgrounds

Columbus Day Festival, San
Francisco.
Reedley Festival.
Chinese Double Ten Celebration, San Francisco.
San Francisco International
Film Festival.
Discovery Day, Bodega Bay.
Harvest Hoedown, Healdsburg.

NOVEMBER

North California Boat and
Sports Show, Oakland.
Christmas Balloon Parade, San
Jose (day after Thanksgiving).
Thanksgiving Art Fair, Mendocino.

DECEMBER

Christmas Art and Music Fes-
tival, Eureka.
Great Dickens Faire, San Francisco.
Nutcracker Suite, San Francisco
Ballet.
Nutcracker Suite, Oakland
Ballet.
Festival of the Trees, Monterey.
Festival of the Trees, San
Rafael.
Shriners East-West Football
Game, Candlestick Park, San
Francisco (December 31).
Lighting of the Tree of Lebanon, Santa Rosa.
New Year's Eve Fireman's Ball,
Cloverdale.
Natives Christmas Tree Ceremony, Sequoia National Forest.
Christmas Tree Lane, Fresno.
Rice-Pounding Ceremony,
Japantown, San Francisco.
Miner's Christmas, Columbia.

INDEX